AFFIRMATIONS

Learn & Implement the Science Behind, Decode & Create Custom Affirmations Following 4 Golden Rules, Avoid Obvious Mistakes, and Get a Bonus of 100 Ready-made Affirmations

By

RHONDA MORRIS

Email: morisrhonda@gmail.com

Website: https://rhondamoris.com

FREE Gift: https://gift.rhondamoris.com

Your FREE GIFT

As an expression of gratitude for investing your time in reading my book, I'd like to extend **a complimentary gift** to you. Get this **eBook** to transform your mindset and attract abundance.

Scan the below QR code to receive _"1000 Affirmations - The Only Book On Affirmations You Need!"_

Thank You, Universe!

I breathe in and fill myself with all the wealth & abundance the Universe has available to me.

WHY SHOULD YOU READ THIS BOOK?

Unlock Your Inner Power, Transform Your Life with Affirmations, and Manifest Your Desires with Certainty!

Are you ready to **transform your life** *and* **unlock your full potential?**

Have you ever wondered how some people seem to **effortlessly achieve their goals** *while others* **struggle** *to progress?*

What if you could grasp the most effective methods embraced by pioneers in affirmations, such **as Louise Hay, Wayne Dyer,** *and* **Deepak Chopra?**

Imagine having **a complete toolbox** filled with empowering affirmations, enabling you to tackle life's challenges with unwavering positivity and clarity.

Dive into the world of affirmations with *"Let's Master Affirmations,"* your ultimate guide to understanding, decoding, and harnessing the true power of affirmations.

What You Get:

- Explore the fascinating **history behind affirmations** and learn why they've become a cornerstone of personal growth and success.

- Learn the **science behind affirmations** and uncover the research supporting their effectiveness.

- Learn about **affirmations' impact on the brain's reward center,** their role in reducing stress, and improving overall well-being. **Gain valuable insights** into why affirmations work.

- Master the <u>**four golden rules**</u> for creating affirmations that evoke positive emotions and align with your deepest desires.

- From gratitude-based affirmations to goal-oriented and action-oriented statements, discover the **diverse range of affirmations** and their unique benefits.

- Identify **common mistakes** hindering your affirmation practice and learn practical strategies to overcome them.

- Learn to incorporate self-affirmations into your **morning routine** and make them a habit.

- Explore a curated list of essential tools and resources to support your affirmation journey, from journals and apps to meditation cushions and more.

- **Bonus Chapter:** Gain access to **100 ready-made affirmations** covering all areas of life, including **health, relationships, career, and money.** Whether you're looking to boost your confidence, attract abundance, or manifest your dreams, these affirmations have you covered.

"Your life is a reflection of your thoughts. Transform your affirmations, transform your world."

- Rhonda Morris

So, are you ready to embark on this life-changing journey?

Keep reading this book...

TABLE OF CONTENTS

INTRODUCTION

"I don't know how, but it'll happen!"

- Rhonda Morris

Photo by Tim Mossholder on Unsplash

IT CHANGED MY LIFE

*S*tarting *my dream business in the **Internet of Things** (IoT) was something I was really passionate about. But even with all the talent, resources, and time on my side, I hesitated to launch my first online course. I was held back by thoughts like "I can't do it alone," "I'm not good enough," and "It needs to be perfect." These doubts filled my mind with worries about failing and wondering if anyone would even be interested in my course.*

I kept getting stuck in a cycle of overthinking and procrastination, which affected my career and stopped me from moving forward. Every time I thought about taking the next step, something held me back, making it hard to make a clear decision about my career.

*Since I was a kid, I've always been curious about the power of the subconscious mind, inner strength, and the impact of our thoughts. Books from authors like **Abraham Hicks, Jack Canfield,** and **Louise Hay** inspired me to learn more about myself, my inner power, and how powerful our thoughts can be.*

*One day, while reading about affirmations and their impact on our lives, I was captivated by the idea and wanted to try them out for myself. That's when I decided to use affirmations to pursue a career in **IoT** more seriously. I started learning more about the topic, how to create effective affirmations, and how to practice them daily.*

*Honestly, at first, I was a bit skeptical about whether affirmations would really work for me. But I didn't let that stop me. I found a mentor to guide me and dove into learning more about the science behind affirmations. I followed a **structured approach** and dedicated myself to self-improvement. Over time, I stopped worrying about the outcomes and began to truly believe in the power of affirmations.*

After about 10-11 months of practicing affirmations consistently, I started noticing positive changes in my life.

At present, my mornings kick off with a routine that sets a positive mood for the rest of my day. I start with gratitude, taking a moment to appreciate the little things in life. Then, I dedicate 15-30 minutes to speaking my affirmations and rewiring my subconscious mind.

My tailored affirmations focused on my IoT career have boosted my confidence and paved the way for my success. My mantra became simple yet powerful: "I don't know how, but it will happen!"

*I noticed that as I continued with this practice, I started to come up with more ideas on how to start my journey, manage stress, and handle criticism. This approach helped me clear out the negativity within me. With the help of affirmations, I took charge of my negative emotions, became self-motivated, and started making decisions that aligned with my career goals. This consistent practice of affirmations elevated my self-motivation, propelling me to launch my **first IoT online course**.*

My newfound confidence was evident to everyone around me during and after the course launch. The course began to gain traction, drawing interest from students worldwide. It was a defining moment for me, where I truly experienced the transformative power of affirmations in action.

Since then, I've made it a point never to skip my morning rituals. Affirmations have become integral to my lifestyle, helping me stay grounded, motivated, and focused on achieving my goals.

IT CAN CHANGE YOURS - *PURPOSE OF WRITING THIS BOOK*

You might be wondering:

- *Do affirmations really work?*

- *Can simply speaking positive words aloud help us achieve our desires?*

- *Can affirmations truly transform our lives?*

There's no need to worry if these questions are on your mind. Just come along with me on this journey. **You'll see the results unfold by following the advice, implementing the strategies, and crafting the right affirmations outlined in this book.**

As **psychologist *Lauren Alexander, PhD,*** suggests, *"In a society where negativity can easily weigh us down, positive affirmations serve as a tool to counter that negativity, reshaping how we talk to ourselves."*

I wrote this book because I've walked in your shoes. I know what it feels like to have big dreams and face self-doubt, to be held back by limiting beliefs and fears of failure. My journey in the Internet of Things (IoT) field taught me the profound impact of our mindset on our ability to achieve our goals.

Through my own experiences, I discovered the incredible power of affirmations in transforming our inner dialogue, boosting our confidence, and reshaping our reality. Believe me, affirmations became my guiding light, helping me break free from self-imposed limitations and take actionable steps toward my dreams, and I am sure it can help you, too.

I wrote this book from the depths of my heart, hoping to reach out and touch your life as affirmations have touched mine. I wish to empower you with the transformative power of positive affirmations, guiding you to reshape your mindset, conquer challenges, and discover your incredible potential.

Whether you're reaching for new heights in your career, seeking to deepen the bonds in your relationships, or aiming to enhance your overall well-being, affirmations can be the **gentle flame that lights up your path**, guiding you toward meaningful and enduring transformation.

This book is a labor of love, crafted with genuine care to accompany you on your personal journey of self-discovery and growth. You'll find not just words but **heartfelt stories, practical wisdom,** and **empowering exercises** meant to guide and inspire you.

I wholeheartedly believe in your potential, and I'm here to remind you that **with the right mindset and tools, you have the power to achieve anything your heart desires. Let's walk this transformative path together, hand in hand, as you uncover the incredible possibilities that await you**.

WHAT TO EXPECT FROM THIS BOOK

In this book, you'll find a warm and inviting guide sharing insights from my life journey, showing you how affirmations can make a difference.

We'll explore key ideas together, diving into the science and heart behind affirmations and how they can shape our mindset and happiness.

- **Personal Insights:** Discover insights from my own life journey, showing you the transformative power of affirmations.

- **Key Concepts:** Explore foundational ideas behind affirmations from a scientific and heartfelt perspective.

- **Practical Exercises:** Engage in hands-on exercises designed to help you craft affirmations tailored to your unique goals and challenges.

Real-Life Stories

- **Inspiring Narratives:** Meet real people with stories that showcase the transformative impact of affirmations in their lives.

Ready-Made Affirmations

- **Daily Inspiration:** Access a collection of ready-to-use affirmations spanning various life areas, offering daily guidance and support.

Measuring Progress and Adjusting Your Approach

- **Track Your Growth:** Utilize tools to measure your progress, helping you stay focused and motivated on your journey.

- **Adaptability:** Learn how to adjust your approach as you grow and evolve, ensuring your affirmations continue to resonate with your changing needs.

Affirmation Templates and Resources

- **Practical Tools:** Find useful templates to help you craft powerful affirmations for different areas of your life.

- **Additional Resources:** Explore a curated list of resources for further practice and deeper exploration of affirmations.

So, dear reader, let's not wait any longer. Join me on this journey as we learn to create personalized affirmations, use them in our daily lives, and pave the way for a brighter future together!

UNDERSTANDING AFFIRMATIONS

"Attitude is a choice. Happiness is a choice. Optimism is a choice. Kindness is a choice. Giving is a choice. Respect is a choice. Whatever choice you make makes you. Choose wisely."

- Roy T. Bennett

Photo by Nathan Dumlao on Unsplash

I remember that once, **Jennifer Lopez** shared her empowering affirmations on Twitter: *"I am whole, I am good on my own, I love myself."*

Similarly, **Michelle Obama** expressed her daily mantra in a tweet, saying, *"Am I good enough? Yes, I am. The mantra I practice daily."*

DECODING AFFIRMATIONS

Affirmations are positive phrases or words that help boost your mood and mindset, like saying, *"I am strong and beautiful."*

You might think of them as similar to **mantras**, which are repeated during meditation to focus the mind. *Mantras* have a long history, especially in **Buddhist** and **Sanskrit** traditions. The word **"mantra"** comes from the *Sanskrit* words *"man,"* to think, and *"tr,"* to liberate, suggesting they help free the mind from negative thoughts.

So, whether through affirmations or *mantras*, the idea is to use positive words and phrases to uplift your spirit and mindset.

When you dissect the word **"Affirmations"**:

- *"Affirm"* comes from the Latin word *"affirmare,"* meaning *"to make firm"* or *"to assert."*

- The suffix *"-ations"* forms nouns indicating actions or processes, such as the process or action of affirming.

So, *"affirmations"* refer to **asserting positive statements to oneself to foster a positive mindset and self-belief.**

For example,

- ***"I am capable and strong."***

This affirmation asserts personal strength and ability. By repeating this phrase, you reinforce the belief in your own capabilities, helping to build confidence and resilience.

- ***"I deserve happiness and success."***

This affirmation emphasizes self-worth and the right to pursue happiness and success. It encourages a positive mindset, reminding you to prioritize your well-being and aspirations.

When you're feeling great about hitting a goal or struggling after a tough day, the words you use with yourself make a big difference.

Do you know this saying: ***"If you can believe it, you can achieve it"?***

That's the core idea behind affirmations - short, positive phrases that help shift your thinking and boost your mood.

If you've tried meditation or yoga, you might have come across affirmations. People often use those uplifting statements to help focus and motivate themselves. These simple sayings can make a big difference in conquering self-doubt, facing fears, and maintaining a positive outlook.

Corey Yeager, *a therapist and author of "How Am I Doing?"*, points out how easy and accessible affirmations are. *"You can use affirmations anywhere, anytime, and they don't cost a thing,"* he says. *"They're a great tool for managing stress and helping yourself out when things get tough."*

So, what exactly are affirmations?

They're positive phrases you can repeat to yourself, either out loud or in your head. These words are meant to lift you up, especially when you're facing challenges. Instead of trying to change your thoughts, the idea is to change how you relate to them.

We all have thousands of thoughts daily, some good and some not-so-good. By paying attention to them without getting caught up in the negative ones, you can start to feel more in control.

It's all about learning to observe your thoughts without letting them bring you down.

According to the **Cleveland Clinic**, when used regularly, affirmations can help shift your mindset from negative to positive. These statements can motivate you, reduce stress, help you through tough times, and boost your confidence and overall well-being.

Lee Phillips, *a psychotherapist from New York City*, agrees that affirmations are a powerful tool for building self-esteem and challenging negative thinking. *"Affirmations can really help replace those negative thoughts with more positive ones, especially when you're dealing with stress, depression, or anxiety,"* he says.

So, how do affirmations do this magic?

Dr. Yeager breaks it down like this: Affirmations work by replacing negative self-talk. For instance, if you mess up and find yourself thinking, **"I'm so stupid,"** that's unintentionally feeding into negative self-talk.

The good news is that you can turn it around once you recognize this negative self-talk. Instead of beating yourself up, you can shift your mindset with a positive affirmation. For example, you might say to yourself, **"I can learn from my mistakes,"** which focuses on growth and learning rather than self-criticism.

Now, let's dive into some psychology behind self-affirmation:

Claude M. Steele, *a social psychologist,* conducted research in the 1980s that sheds light on this topic. Steele's theory suggests that when people face situations or thoughts that challenge how they see themselves, they're driven to restore their self-image.

Essentially, we all want to see ourselves in a positive light. So, when faced with a threat to our self-image, like someone saying we're not good at something, we naturally seek ways to reaffirm our self-worth. This self-affirmation helps us manage these challenges with more confidence and balance. Think of it as your personal guide for facing challenges—it's about strengthening a positive view of yourself to help you through tough times.

AFFIRMATIONS CHANGED HER LIFE

Once, there was a young singer who dreamed of shining in an audition. But her confidence was weighed down by past failures. She had doubts creeping into her mind, dragging her confidence down like anchors.

She had something special inside—a voice that could make people feel things. But she often doubted herself, wondering if others would approve. She worried, *"What if they don't like me? What if I fail again?"*

She knew she needed to do something different, so she began to explore herself. She found peace in using affirmations, simple words that could change her life.

Each day, she sat quietly for a moment. With her eyes closed and body relaxed, she repeated positive statements to herself:

"I have a beautiful voice. People love my singing. I am already getting compliments for my talent. I am being asked to audition and get good feedback. I am getting chances to talk on TV and social media. I am a successful singer!"

Each time she repeated the affirmations, she felt more confident. Gradually, the positive words helped her believe in herself.

After a month, she felt completely different. She was full of confidence and determination as she prepared for the audition. When she sang, her voice touched everyone in the room. Her performance was so impressive that it left everyone stunned.

So, why did it work after a month when it had not worked before?

It worked because she chose to believe in herself. She rewired her mindset by consistently repeating positive affirmations, replacing self-doubt with confidence. Through dedication and perseverance, she unlocked the potential within her, allowing her true talent to shine brightly. And when she faced the audition with a newfound sense of purpose, her belief in herself resonated with everyone who listened, leaving an indelible mark on their hearts. Her faith in her abilities ultimately propelled her toward success, proving that anything is possible with dedication, positivity, and self-belief.

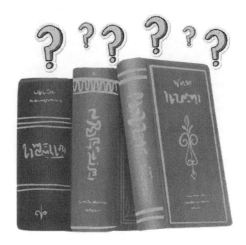

Affirmations have been around for a long time and are found in many different cultures and religions.

Whether it's saying positive prayers in Christianity or using chants in Hinduism, people have believed in **the power of words** to bring about positive change for centuries.

In the **1800s**, a *French psychologist and pharmacist* named **Emile Coue** came up with a new way to help people improve themselves. He called it **"conscious autosuggestion."**

This method involved repeating positive phrases or affirmations to help people feel better and make positive changes in their lives.

One of his most famous phrases was, *"Every day, in every way, I am getting better and better."*

People really liked this idea and found it helpful for personal growth and self-improvement.

Coue thought that **what we imagine can really affect how our bodies feel, even more than just trying hard.** He believed that **by repeating positive thoughts, our bodies would start to feel better, too.** This was a new idea at the time, as most people were focused on looking at problems rather than thinking positively.

After Coue's ideas became popular, a movement called **New Thought** took off in the early 1900s. Leaders like **Charles** and **Myrtle Fillmore,** who started **Unity Church,** believed that we all have great potential and that our thoughts can improve our lives. They **encouraged people to use positive affirmations to bring more health, happiness, and success into their lives**.

This movement changed how people thought about improving themselves. It showed that people could improve their lives by thinking positively. **Affirmations went from being just a way to boost mood to being seen as a path to both spiritual growth and real-world success.**

Thanks to Coue and the New Thought movement, we now see affirmations as a helpful tool for making positive changes in our lives. Today, many people use affirmations in self-help methods and wellness routines to improve different parts of their lives.

THE RISE OF AFFIRMATIONS

In the late 20th century, more people began to discover affirmations, and a significant influence behind this was the late **Louise Hay**.

She was an author and speaker who had faced tough challenges, including abuse and illness. Louise believed that positive thinking and using affirmations played a key role in her healing journey. Her book, ***"You Can Heal Your Life,"*** published in 1984, introduced many to the concept of affirmations.

In her book, Louise explained how our thoughts and words can shape our lives and offered specific affirmations to address various health issues. She emphasized that **negative beliefs in our minds can impact our well-being**.

Louise's insights resonated with many, making her book a bestseller. Thanks to her impactful contributions, Louise became a respected figure in the wellness and self-help community.

Dear reader, I hope you've gained a good understanding of affirmations—what they are and how they can be beneficial in our lives. As we've journeyed through their history and rise to popularity, you might be curious about the science behind their effectiveness.

In the next chapter, we'll explore why affirmations work and the research and evidence supporting their impact on personal growth and well-being. **Stay with me as we uncover the fascinating science behind the power of positive affirmations.**

- Affirmations are positive statements that make us feel better and help us stay positive, especially when things are tough.

- People from different cultures and religions have used affirmations for a long time. Recently, famous people like Louise Hay have made them more popular.

- Affirmations are like tools we can use anytime to feel better and deal with problems. They help us feel good about ourselves and think more positively.

- Affirmations can help us feel more confident and strong when we face challenges.

WHY AFFIRMATIONS WORK - *LET ME PROVE!*

"Affirmation without discipline is the beginning of delusion."

- *Jim Rohn*

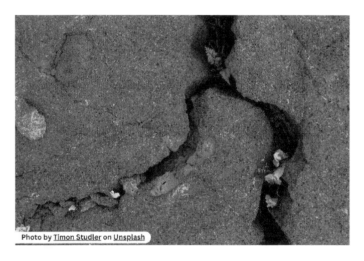

Photo by <u>Timon Studler</u> on <u>Unsplash</u>

*F*eeling *worn out, lacking motivation, or worrying about what's ahead?*

You're not alone. Even successful people, like celebrities and life coaches, have these moments. But remember, **it's just a phase,** and **there's a way to turn things around** by aligning your energy with the **Universe**.

So, what do I mean by ***aligning your energy with the Universe?***

Let's not complicate things. The simple meaning is that ***by focusing on positive thoughts and actions, you can improve your situation and feel more in tune with the world around you.***

I remember when I started my online IoT course, I felt overwhelmed and kept telling myself, *"If I don't do it, no one else will."* And guess what? That negative thinking became a reality. I took on more than I could handle and didn't ask for help. It wasn't until I changed my mindset to focus on positive thoughts that I broke free from this cycle.

So, how do you get back on track?

Start by recognizing the power of your thoughts. Every thought you have sends energy out into the Universe, and it responds in kind. If you're stuck in negative or fearful thinking, you'll notice those vibes everywhere around you.

Believe me, dear reader, shifting your energy isn't as hard as it seems. **By picking up this book, you're signaling the Universe that you're open to change.** To keep this momentum going, try making positive thinking a daily habit.

AFFIRMATIONS CHANGED HER LIFE, AND WE BOTH WON THE GAME

A few years ago, I met a lady from New Jersey, USA. She seemed to have everything—a loving husband, two lovely daughters, and a good job at an insurance company. But when we talked, she shared some heavy stuff. She had a skin condition called Rosacea that made her face red and rash. And she didn't like her body because she was too skinny. This made her avoid going out and even looking at herself in the mirror. She told me it's been a long time since she looked at herself in the mirror. She was scared to see herself in it.

Because of all this, she was heartbroken most of the time. She often felt depressed and had panic attacks. She also felt ashamed of being underweight. It made her sad when her old clothes didn't fit her anymore. All of this just added to her distress.

After listening to her for a while, I realized her main problem was that she didn't feel good about herself. So, we decided to work together. We met twice a week for about an hour or so. I wanted to **change her thinking from *"I am not beautiful"* to *"I am the most beautiful lady on earth."*** In every meeting, we mainly focused on improving self-talk and self-love through affirmations.

I gave her simple sentences to repeat daily, like:

- *I am the most lovable person on this planet.*

- *I love myself just the way I am regardless of who loves me or doesn't.*

- *I have already gained weight up to 150 pounds in the last month, and now I am taking care of my health. I love eating healthy food and exercising every day.*

- *I have healthy, thick hair and beautiful, glowing skin. My body is like a temple, and I love caring for it.*

- *I am the best at what I feel, think, believe, or do.*

We also practiced looking in the mirror and saying nice things about herself.

And guess what?

After about four months of working together, she was like a whole new person. She looked healthier, felt more confident, and started going out with her friends again. But the best part was seeing her smile when she looked in the mirror.

It wasn't just a win for her; it was a win for both of us!

DON'T UNDERESTIMATE YOURSELF

When I launched my **IoT online course**, I was overwhelmed with doubts and kept telling myself, *"If I don't make it perfect, no one will be interested."* As a result, I hesitated to promote it and lacked confidence in my own product. Predictably, the course didn't get the attention it deserved, and enrollments were low.

However, my mindset shifted when I changed my approach and focused on positive affirmations. I started believing in the value of my course and the effort I had put into it. I began enthusiastically promoting it, sharing its benefits and why I was passionate about it.

The change was noticeable. Students started showing interest, and enrollments began to increase. The positive energy and belief I put into promoting my course attracted a similar response from others, leading to better outcomes.

So, what is the moral of the story?

You have the ability to change anything in your life right now. With the right mindset, you can turn your dreams into reality. This is where **affirmations** come in, rooted in two key beliefs that have been around for ages:

1. The Law of Oneness and

2. The Law of Attraction

The Law of Oneness teaches us that everything in the Universe originates from the same energy. This interconnectedness means that our actions, thoughts, and emotions can influence everything around us and vice versa.

For example,

Think of a pond with ripples spreading out from a single pebble thrown into it. The pebble represents your actions or thoughts, and the ripples are the effects they have on the pond, which can be seen as everything around you.

On the other hand, **the Law of Attraction** tells us that similar energies attract each other. So, the energy you put out into the world—whether positive or negative—will attract similar energy back to you. So, if you focus on positive thoughts, you'll attract positive outcomes; if you dwell on negative thoughts, you'll attract negative experiences.

For example,

Imagine you wake up feeling grumpy and think, *"Today is going to be a bad day."* Throughout the day, you might notice more things going wrong or people being rude to you. On the other hand, if you wake up feeling positive and think, *"Today is going to be a great day,"* you might notice more good things happening around you, like finding a parking spot easily or receiving compliments from others.

FULLY BACKED UP BY THE SCIENCE & RESEARCH

Scientific research backs up what many people have already found to be true through personal experience: **affirmations can make a real difference in our lives.**

Studies show that regularly practicing affirmations can positively change our mindset, emotions, and even our physical well-being. This growing body of research supports the idea that using affirmations can be a beneficial tool for improving our overall quality of life.

Please allow me to explain a few key studies and the science behind affirmations that will help you understand the deep workings of affirmations and their impact on our lives.

- **SELF-AFFIRMATIONS & THE INTEGRITY OF THE SELF**

A **report** about self-affirmations was published in **Science Direct** by **Claude M. Steele,** *PhD, a social psychologist*.

Self-affirmation theory suggests that when we focus on values that are important to us, we're better able to handle stressful situations and negative information without getting defensive.

The research has shown that practicing self-affirmation can help us deal with challenges, improve our performance in school or work, boost our health, and reduce defensive reactions.

According to **Claude, When we face information that challenges our confidence or sense of self, our minds naturally kick into gear to restore that confidence. We do this by reassuring ourselves through explanations or actions. This ongoing process helps us maintain a positive view of ourselves, seeing ourselves as competent, good, and capable of making choices and controlling outcomes.**

- **POSITIVE AFFIRMATIONS & SUCCESS**

Affirmations are backed by solid science, particularly through a method called **neuro-linguistic programming (NLP).** This approach was developed in the 1970s by *neuroscientists* **John Grinder** and **Richard Bandler** from the *University of Santa Cruz.*

They studied successful psychotherapists and found that success often comes from increasing positive behaviors and reducing negative ones. They also looked at the work of linguists like **Alfred Korzybski** and **Noam Chomsky** to understand language patterns that can limit our understanding and potential for change.

To put it simply, think of negative thought patterns as invisible fences. Just like an electronic barrier keeps a dog in the yard, these negative patterns can hold us back from breaking old habits and trying new things. **By using affirmations and changing our mindset, we can start to break through these invisible barriers and expand our possibilities**.

- **AFFIRMATIONS & HEALTH**

Research shows that positive affirmations can benefit our mental health and overall well-being. **Dr. Sam Zand, *a clinical psychiatrist*** from ***Boise, Idaho,*** explains that affirmations can be helpful because of a concept called **Neuroplasticity**. According to the **information** published in **Frontiers in Psychology**, Neuroplasticity is the brain's ability to create new patterns and adapt.

Dr. Zand compares it to muscle memory: **just like we can train our muscles through repeated exercises, we can also train our brains through consistent affirmation practice**. Instead of reinforcing negative thoughts, we can build a habit of focusing on positive and balanced self-perceptions.

And here is **another research**:

In a study involving women who were worried about their weight, researchers found that self-affirmation can make a real difference. Weight concerns can lead to stress, unhealthy eating habits, and weight gain. Half of the women in the study wrote essays about their core values, which is a form of self-affirmation. The results showed that these women lost more weight, had a lower body mass index (BMI), and smaller waist sizes compared to those who didn't do the self-affirmation exercise.

In **another study,** patients with end-stage renal disease were examined to see how self-affirmation could affect their adherence to phosphate binders, which help control phosphate levels in the body. Poor control of phosphate levels can be dangerous for these patients. The study found that the patients who practiced self-affirmation significantly improved their phosphate levels, indicating better adherence to their medication than those who didn't.

These studies highlight self-affirmation's power in improving physical health, like weight management and medication adherence, which can be crucial for managing serious health conditions.

- **AFFIRMATIONS & YOUR BRAIN'S REWARD CENTER**

According to a **study** published in the **National Library of Medicine** by the **NIH**, researchers used **fMRI** scans to see how affirmations impact the brain's internal processes and reward systems. These scans help show what brain parts are active when doing tasks or feeling emotions.

The study found that people who practiced positive affirmations related to their personal values showed more activity in the brain's reward center. This area is linked to positive self-perception and confidence. In simple terms, affirmations can actually change how our brain responds, boosting feelings of self-worth and competence.

In a study on self-affirmation's impact on stress, college students were asked to participate in a stress test called the **Trier Social Stress Test.** This test is designed to make people feel stressed out. First, the students had to give a short speech in front of judges who didn't give them any feedback or encouragement. Then, they had to do a challenging math task where they counted backward from 2,083 by 13s while being pressured by the judges to go faster.

Before taking this stress test, half of the students were asked to do a self-affirmation exercise. In this exercise, they had to think about and write down their personal values, like what's important to them in life.

After completing the stress test, researchers measured the students' cortisol levels, a hormone released when we're stressed. The results showed that the students who did the self-affirmation exercise had lower cortisol levels than those who didn't. This means that thinking about their values helped reduce their stress during challenging tasks.

In **another study**, students were tested two weeks before a midterm exam to measure their stress hormone levels. Half of them wrote two values essays during this time as a self-affirmation exercise. The results showed that students who didn't do the self-affirmation had increased stress hormone levels leading up to the exam, while those who did the self-affirmation didn't show this increase. This suggests that self-affirmation can help reduce stress levels during challenging times, like preparing for exams.

- **AFFIRMATIONS IN GAMES**

Yeager uses affirmations to help NBA players stay positive and focused during games in his work as a **psychotherapist**

47

for the **Detroit Pistons**. For instance, when a player makes a mistake, like turning over the ball, Yeager encourages them to see it differently. Instead of getting caught up in negativity, they can use affirmations to boost their confidence and resilience.

He suggests an example of an affirmation: *"I was built for this. I'm not worried."* This helps the players shake off mistakes and stay mentally strong throughout the game.

- **SELF-AFFIRMATIONS & YOUR BRAIN**

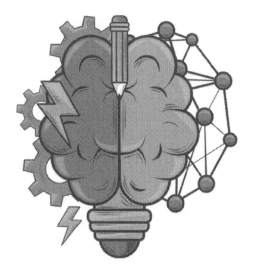

Self-affirmation theory has sparked interest in how our brain responds when we engage in positive self-affirmation. MRI studies have shown that certain parts of our brain become more active when we think about our personal values. Specifically, the **ventromedial prefrontal cortex**, which is involved in positive thinking and processing information about ourselves, lights up when we focus on our values.

A **study** in the journal **"Social Cognitive and Affective Neuroscience"** examined how self-affirmation affects our brain. The researchers found that practicing self-affirmation activates a part of the brain that is linked to feelings of reward and value. So, when we affirm positive beliefs about ourselves, our brain rewards us by activating these pleasure pathways. This reinforces our positive beliefs and encourages us to continue behaving positively.

Similarly, **Dr. Ethan Kross** and his team at the *University of Michigan* have researched **self-talk**, which is closely related to affirmations. Self-talk is the internal conversation we have with ourselves. It's a powerful tool that shapes how we see the world and how we behave. Positive self-talk can boost our confidence, help us handle challenges better, and even improve our overall well-being.

- **SELF-AFFIRMATION AND OPEN-MINDEDNESS**

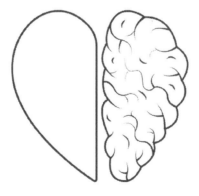

Research has shown that when people engage in activities that boost their self-worth or self-integrity, they become less defensive. This means they're more open to accepting information, even if it challenges their beliefs or opinions. It's like a shield of confidence that makes them more receptive to different perspectives.

It is found that people tend to be more open-minded after completing a self-affirmation task. They're more willing to consider ideas or viewpoints that might differ or even conflict with their own. This shift in mindset suggests that affirming our self-worth can make us more flexible and understanding.

- **SELF-AFFIRMATIONS IN EDUCATION**

Self-affirmations have emerged as a promising tool to boost academic performance, particularly among students who face significant challenges in their school environments. Researchers have been keenly interested in understanding how affirming one's values and self-worth can positively impact the grades of historically marginalized groups, such as African-American and Latino-American students.

According to a report from **PositivePsychology**, participants were divided into two groups in a compelling two-year study involving seventh-grade students. One group was tasked with writing about their most important values several times throughout the study, while the other group focused on why a less important value could be meaningful to someone else. The researchers then closely monitored the student's academic performance over the next three years.

The results were enlightening. Students from ethnic minority backgrounds who engaged in the self-affirmation exercise showed noticeable improvements in their grades compared to their peers who didn't participate in the activity.

Surprisingly, this positive effect of self-affirmation wasn't observed among white students. These findings suggest that for students who regularly face challenges and stressors in their educational journey, affirming their self-worth can act as a protective shield, helping them maintain and even improve their academic performance.

Extending the benefits of self-affirmation further, similar positive outcomes were observed among college students from low socioeconomic backgrounds and women enrolled in introductory physics courses. This highlights the universal potential of self-affirmation to bridge academic achievement gaps, offering a ray of hope for students who face the most challenges in their educational pursuits.

In essence, these studies underscore the transformative power of self-affirmation in education.

After learning from various research and studies, let me take you to the biology of affirmations and explain how our brain, conscious mind, and subconscious minds are connected and work when we affirm something.

CONSCIOUS MIND, SUB-CONSCIOUS MIND AND AFFIRMATIONS

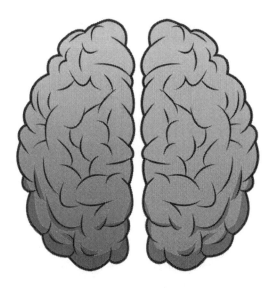

Our **conscious mind** is the part of our brain that we're aware of and actively use throughout the day. It's where we make decisions, solve problems, and interact with the world around us.

Think of it as the captain steering the ship, making day-to-day choices based on our immediate perceptions and understanding.

On the other hand, our **subconscious mind** operates behind the scenes, storing memories, beliefs, and past experiences that shape our behaviors and reactions.

It's like the crew members who work tirelessly below deck, influencing the ship's direction based on their collective experiences.

Now, where do affirmations come into play?

Affirmations act as **powerful messages that we send from our conscious mind to our subconscious mind**.

When we repeat positive affirmations, we're essentially **reprogramming our subconscious beliefs**. Over time, these affirmations can help shift negative or limiting beliefs into more positive, empowering ones.

Imagine your subconscious mind as a vast library filled with books of beliefs and experiences. Some of these books might be outdated or hold negative narratives about ourselves. Affirmations serve as new chapters, rewriting these stories with positive, uplifting messages. As we consistently use affirmations, these new chapters become integrated into our subconscious, influencing our thoughts, feelings, and actions in a positive way.

I define affirmations as *a tool that bridges the gap between our conscious and subconscious minds, allowing us to align our thoughts and beliefs with our goals and aspirations*.

For example,

Imagine you're developing an IoT (Internet of Things) course, much like I did. In the beginning, doubts and uncertainties might cloud your mind. Thoughts like, *"Can I really do this?"* or *"What if it doesn't meet expectations?"* might surface, echoing in your conscious and subconscious minds.

This is where affirmations can come to your rescue. By crafting positive affirmations like, *"I have the knowledge and skills to create an impactful IoT course,"* or *"Every challenge I face is an opportunity to learn and grow,"* you can actively shift these doubts.

I exactly did this to overcome my limiting beliefs in the past.

As I repeated these affirmations, I wasn't just telling my conscious mind to stay focused and sending reassuring messages to my subconscious.

Over time, these consistent affirmations transformed my doubts into confidence, pushing me forward with renewed determination and clarity. As a result, I successfully launched my IoT course.

So, just as affirmations helped me navigate the challenges of launching my IoT course, they can also guide you in aligning your conscious and subconscious minds toward your goals.

As we wrap up this chapter, I hope you've gained valuable insights from the scientific evidence and studies supporting the power of affirmations.

Feeling convinced that affirmations can truly benefit you?

Great!

But you might wonder, **_how do you craft effective affirmations that deliver results?_**

If that's on your mind, you're in the right place!

Stay with me because, in the next chapter, we'll dive into creating decisive, effective affirmations step by step.

Get ready to transform your mindset!

- Everyone experiences moments of doubt and worry, even successful individuals.

- Aligning your energy with the Universe involves focusing on positive thoughts and actions.

- Focusing on positive thoughts and actions can improve your situation and make you feel more connected to the world around you.

- Recognizing the influence of your thoughts on your reality empowers you to shift from negative to positive thinking, thereby altering your outcomes.

- Embracing the idea that you have the ability to change your life right now by adopting a positive mindset and utilizing affirmations.

- The Law of Oneness and the Law of Attraction underscore how our thoughts and actions influence the world around us and shape our reality.

- Numerous studies support the efficacy of affirmations in improving mindset, emotional well-being, physical health, academic performance, and stress management, offering concrete evidence of their effectiveness.

LET'S LEARN TO CRAFT THE MOST POWERFUL AFFIRMATIONS

"Daily affirmations are like a tonic for your soul."

- *Rhonda Morris*

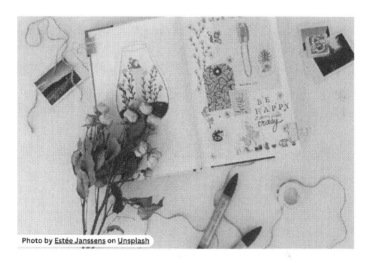

Photo by Estée Janssens on Unsplash

*H*ere is the story of a young man who felt really sad because his girlfriend had left him. She went away with another guy and took his money, leaving him with nothing. It hurt him so much that he felt like he lost a piece of himself. He didn't know what to do with all the sadness, and it made it hard for him to do his job or even eat. He loved her a lot, and it hurt him even more because he trusted her with his heart. He couldn't understand why she would hurt him like that.

One day, he decided to try something different.

Even though forgiving her seemed impossible, he wanted to give it a shot. He hoped that maybe forgiving her would make the pain disappear, even slightly. Instead of saying the words, he did something else. He changed his phone password to **"i4giveyou."** Every time he unlocked his phone, he saw those words.

As days went by, something surprising happened. He started to feel a tiny bit better. The anger and sadness didn't weigh him down as much. It was like a little ray of hope shining through the dark clouds of his heart. He realized that forgiving her, even if just a little bit, helped him find a little bit of peace inside himself.

He learned that saying positive things, even when it's hard, can change how you feel. And by forgiving, he set himself free from the pain of the past, ready to move forward with a little bit of hope in his heart.

The moral?

The moral of the story is that even when you feel hurt, saying positive things to yourself can help you feel better. As you see, the young man changed his phone password to "i4giveyou" to remind himself to forgive his girlfriend. Even though it was hard, it eventually helped him feel some peace. So, the moral is that using affirmations, like saying kind things to yourself, can help you heal from painful experiences and move forward with hope.

In my webinars, I've been spending a lot of time discussing how to create affirmations step-by-step. Despite providing specific guidance, I still find that some people are unsure if their affirmations are effective. They often come back to me seeking validation, asking, *"Is this affirmation right or wrong?"*

To address this, I've developed a straightforward formula for crafting affirmations. It's designed to be incredibly simple, practical, and yet surprisingly powerful.

You see, one of the main reasons people struggle with affirmations is because they can seem daunting and unfamiliar. It's like they're this mysterious, scientific concept that's hard to grasp.

But the truth is, affirmations are just like having a conversation with yourself. They're about speaking to yourself in a positive and empowering way. So, instead of thinking of them as some complex concept, let's reframe it and call it what it really is: **a conversation.**

When you think of affirmations as conversations, it becomes much easier to understand and implement them in your daily life.

Just like you'd have a chat with a friend to uplift them, affirmations are a way to uplift yourself and shift your mindset towards positivity and self-belief. It's a simple shift in perspective that can make a world of difference in how you approach affirmations.

So, what's a conversation?

It's simply talking to someone, right?

Like how I'm talking to you now, well, guess what? When you have a chat with your friend, that's actually a form of affirmation, too. Let me explain.

Affirmations work on a simple formula: feel, think, believe, and act as if you already have what you desire. That's the **FTBA formula - Feel, Think, Believe,** and **Act.** For me, it's about feeling, thinking, believing, and acting as if I already have what I want.

Here's how it works: When you start saying things as if you already have what you desire, you're basically aligning your vibes with your goal. And when your vibes match your goal vibes, that's when the magic of attraction kicks in automatically. It's like tuning into the same frequency, and bam — things start falling into place.

But how do you get on the same frequency as your goal? Well, there are plenty of ways to do it, but one of the most powerful techniques is through affirmations (conversations).

Let me break it down for you with an example-

Let's say you want to visualize yourself chilling at **Bal Harbour Beach** in **Miami**. Many folks might start their affirmation like this: *"Thank you, Universe (or God), I've reached Bal Harbour, and I'm so happy right now."*

Sounds good, right?

But hold on—what's missing here? Can you guess?

Here's the thing: Many people forget a crucial component - **"elaborated feelings."**

Imagine you've achieved something amazing in your life, and you're bursting to share the news with your best friend. What kind of **conversation** would you have about it? You'd probably dive into every little detail and be super excited, and your expressions would say it all, right? You'd use phrases like, *"You know, I've achieved this... I already have it now... I'm really enjoying the moment..."*

That **"conversation"** with your friend is essentially an **affirmation** in that scenario. It's about expressing your feelings and thoughts as if you've already achieved your goal. That's where the real power lies.

Now, let's think about this with a couple of examples.

Imagine you want to tie the knot, and you're excitedly sharing the news with your bestie. You might say something like, *"Guess what? I actually got married last night (or last week or last month), and I'm over the moon with my life partner. We're having the time of our lives together."*

Sounds like a typical conversation you'd have with your best friend, right? Well, guess what? **That's also an affirmation.**

Here's **another example.**

Imagine you've been away for a while and are finally back home. You can't wait to share some exciting news with your mom. You might say, *"Mom, I've got something amazing to tell you. I actually finished writing my book three months ago, and I'm thrilled about it. Since then, I've been getting such positive feedback from readers, and it's been a dream come true."*

See?

It's like having a casual chat with your mom but also a way of affirming your success and happiness.

So, here's the bottom line for creating affirmations: **Keep it practical and straightforward. That's the golden rule**.

Imagine you're an artist about to create a masterpiece. But before you start, you need to know what you want to create. It's like looking at a blank canvas or a block of clay before it becomes a beautiful painting or sculpture.

Similarly, in life, you need to have a clear vision of what you want. So, take a moment to think deeply about what you desire most.

Take a moment to get comfy, close your eyes, and breathe deeply. Imagine a warm, glowing light wrapping around you, spreading out into the big, wide Universe. Now, deep down in your heart, ask yourself what you really, really want...

If that feels tough, try **breaking things down into sections like your friendships, hobbies, health, and how you feel about each part of your life? Take a moment to think about what could use a little sprinkle of improvement**.

Once you've got a good idea, write down your desires as if they've already come true. Keep it positive because the Universe listens to what you focus on. So, instead of saying what you don't want, say what you do want.

For instance, instead of saying, *"I want to stop having bad luck with dating,"* say, *"I am in a loving relationship."* This positive energy will help bring your desires to life.

Alright, now that you've got a goal in your sights, let's flesh it out a bit. Adding details to your goal does wonders. It stirs up feelings, gets your brain buzzing, and even taps into your subconscious to make things happen. See, your subconscious is a big player in bringing your dreams to life. Sometimes, it even has more influence than your conscious thoughts.

But don't worry, you're not powerless against it. You can train your subconscious with a bit of practice.

Need proof? Try this neat trick.

*Picture yourself walking barefoot on a sandy beach at sunset. You reach down and pick up a seashell, feeling its smooth surface in your hand. Bring it close to your ear and listen to the gentle sound of the ocean. **Though it's just in your mind, your senses might react as if you're truly there**.*

So, why not use this power of imagination to make your dreams a reality?

That's where the **"mental snapshot"** comes in.

Think about your goal and paint a detailed picture in your mind. Picture where you'll be, what you'll wear, and who might be there with you. Dive deep into the scene. Imagine the smells, the sounds, the sensations. Let it all sink in.

Pay attention to how it makes you feel. If any negativity creeps in, tweak your mental picture until it's all positive vibes.

Then, whenever you revisit this mental snapshot, make sure to amp up those good feelings. Trust me; it'll help pave the way for your dreams to come true.

LET YOUR VISION TAKE FLIGHT

Ever felt that peaceful drift just before sleep takes over?

Well, that's what scientists call **the alpha state**. It's when your brain waves slow down a bit, setting the stage for what you want to happen next. See, your subconscious is most open to messages when your brain's chilling in alpha mode. So, **the better you get at slipping into this relaxed state, the better your affirmations will work**.

Here's another exercise to help you relax and tap into your inner calm:

Take a seat in a comfy chair or lie down somewhere cozy. Close your eyes gently and begin to tune in to your breath. Feel the air flowing in and out of your lungs. Let your breathing find its natural rhythm, like gentle waves lapping at the shore.

Now, imagine a warm, soothing light hovering above your head. With each inhale, feel this light gently descending, wrapping around the top of your head like a comforting blanket. As it moves down, allow it to melt away any tension in your scalp, forehead, and temples.

Continue to breathe deeply and slowly as the light travels down your face, softening your jaw, relaxing your cheeks, and releasing any tightness around your eyes. Feel the warmth spreading down your neck and shoulders, loosening knots and easing stiffness.

With each breath, let the light flow down through your arms, all the way to your fingertips, leaving behind a sense of calm and tranquility. Then, guide it down through your chest and torso, soothing your heart and belly and grounding you in a deep sense of peace.

As the light reaches your hips, thighs, and knees, feel any remaining tension melting away, allowing you to sink deeper into relaxation. Finally, let it flow down through your calves, ankles, and feet, leaving you feeling completely relaxed and at ease.

Now, **remember that vivid "mental snapshot" you painted earlier?**

Bring it back. Feel all the good vibes that come with it. Here's a little trick to supercharge this exercise: imagine you're watching yourself in that scene like an observer. Capture this moment like a mental photo and pin it to your life's timeline.

Finally, **show the Universe a heartfelt "thank you" and let your vision take flight**.

Now that you've got your **mental snapshot** and feel positive about affirmations, let's dive into the fundamental rules.

To make effective affirmations and to affirm them correctly, we must follow the below FOUR rules-

- **RULE #1: SPECIFIC END RESULT**

When you're making affirmations, it's important to be specific about what you want. Being specific means **being clear and exact about your goal**.

For example, instead of saying,

"I want to become slim," which is a bit vague; you could say something like,

"I want to weigh 143 pounds."

Why is being specific important?

Well, when you're clear about your goal, it's easier for your mind to focus on achieving it. It's like having a map to follow rather than wandering around aimlessly.

Here's another thing to remember: Don't worry too much about how you'll reach your goal.

Sometimes, we get caught up in the details of the process, like thinking we need to walk for an hour every day to lose weight. But really, what matters is the end result – in this case, reaching a weight of 143 pounds irrespective of any means.

So, instead of saying something like,

"I want to weigh 143 pounds by walking every day for an hour," you could simply say,

"I want to weigh 143 pounds."

That way, you're focusing on the outcome you want to achieve without getting bogged down in the specifics of how you'll get there.

- **RULE #2: KEEP IN MIND THAT YOU HAVE ALREADY ACHIEVED THEM**

When you're making affirmations, it's important to talk about your goals as if they've already happened.

Instead of saying,

"I will reduce my body weight to 143 pounds by 16th Aug 2025," or *"I want to reduce my body weight to 143 pounds by 16th Aug 2025,"* you'd say something like,

"Today is 20th Oct 2025, and I've already reduced my body weight to 143 pounds two months ago."

Why do we do this?

Talking about your goals as if they've already come true helps you believe they're possible. It's like tricking your brain into thinking it's already happened, making it easier to stay motivated and focused on reaching your goal.

Here's another reason: You don't want to get too caught up in the excitement of achieving your goal. If you talk about it like it just happened or like you're in the process of making it happen right now, your emotions might go into overdrive. We can't sustain that level of excitement all the time.

So, when framing your affirmations, try to keep your emotions in check. Instead of getting overly excited, aim for a more balanced emotional state.

For example, you could say,

"Today is 20th Oct 2022, and I've already reduced my body weight to 143 pounds two months ago. Thank you, Universe; I feel contented and satisfied!"

This way, you're acknowledging your achievement while also staying grounded.

- **RULE #3: ADD POSITIVE EMOTIONAL WORDS TO YOUR AFFIRMATIONS**

When you're saying your affirmations, bring some positive vibes into it!

Imagine how you'd feel when you reach your goals and thank the Universe. You'd probably feel happy, satisfied, peaceful, strong, secure, complete, right? So, when you're making your affirmations, include these good feelings.

For instance, instead of saying,

"Today is 31st Dec 2026, and I already have 15 multiple sources of income," you could say,

"Today is 31st Dec 2026, and I already have 15 multiple sources of income. Thank you, Universe, for making me feel secure and satisfied!"

This way, you're not only stating your achievement but also acknowledging how good it makes you feel.

- **RULE #4: CREATE THE FEELINGS FIRST, THEN SAY YOUR AFFIRMATIONS**

This rule isn't about making your affirmations but about how you say them.

It's super important, so heads up!

Instead of waiting to feel energetic after saying your affirmations, you gotta create that energy first.

Yes, you heard that right!

Get yourself pumped up before you say your affirmations. Then, when you're all pumped up, let those affirmations out with that same high energy. This makes them way more powerful and effective.

Now, you might wonder, how do you get yourself all pumped up? Right?

It's easy! Just put on some music and move your body for about 5 minutes. You know, dance around a bit! Once you're feeling energized, that's when you should say your affirmations.

3 TYPES OF AFFIRMATIONS

Let's break down the different types of affirmations we should prepare for our goals.

- **#1: THANK YOU - AFFIRMATIONS**

First up, we've got **"thank you-affirmations."**

These are like **gratitude affirmations** for our goals. We also call them **"maintenance frequency affirmations."** With these affirmations, we're thanking the Universe for everything we already have. It's about appreciating what's already in our lives and keeping that positive energy going.

For example:

- *Thank you, Universe, for giving me stamina, thick hair, and beautiful glowing skin!*

- *Thank you, Universe, for allowing our parents to live with us and blessing us with their love daily!*

- *Thank you, Universe, for helping me complete my Oracle certification last week!*

- *Thank you, Universe, for providing me with all the income sources I already have.*

- *Thank you, Universe, for the successful webinar I delivered today on "Self-motivation."*

These affirmations help us stay grateful and maintain the good things we already have in our lives.

- **#2: GOAL FREQUENCY-AFFIRMATIONS**

These affirmations are all about the actual goals you really want to achieve. But you have to do these as you've already achieved them, just like we discussed earlier.

For example:

- *Today is 20th Oct 2025, and I've already reduced my body weight to 143 pounds two months ago.*

See, you're talking about your goal like it's already happened. This helps your brain believe it's possible and gets you in the right mindset to make it a reality.

Cool, right?

- **#3: ACTION FREQUENCY-AFFIRMATIONS**

These affirmations are all about the actions you need to take to reach your goals. They're like little reminders to yourself about the things you gotta do. When you're making these affirmations, try to use action verbs to make them more powerful.

For example:

- *I love eating healthy food and exercising.*

- *Thank you, Universe, for helping me treat my body like a temple and for loving to take care of my health!*

- *I love studying the AWS certification guide and spend two hours daily doing the hands-on practice.*

- *I love delivering 10x value to all my clients and students.*

See how these affirmations are all about the actions you're gonna take? They're like little pep talks to keep you on track and motivated.

LET'S HAVE SOME SAMPLE AFFIRMATIONS

Allow me to share a few of my affirmations that I repeat daily. They're like little sparks of positivity fueling my day, and they might inspire you to create your own!

For my "weight loss" goal:

- *Thank you, Universe, for filling me with happiness, positivity, and satisfaction every single day!*

- *Thank you for blessing me with rock-solid immune and digestive systems that work like a charm!*

- *Today is 20th Oct 2025, and I'm thrilled to say that I've already shed those extra pounds, reaching my goal of 143 pounds two months ago. I'm feeling incredibly content and satisfied!*

- *I absolutely adore my daily exercise routine and the refreshing walks I take. Thank you for giving me the energy and motivation to keep moving!*

- *Thank you for the delicious and nutritious food I enjoy every day. Eating healthy feels amazing!*

For "the time I spend with my family":

- *Thank you, Universe, for the precious gift of family. I am beyond grateful for their presence in my life!*

- *Spending quality time with my loved ones fills my heart with joy and warmth.*

- *Today is 16th Mar 2025, and I'm overflowing with happiness because I now get to spend quality time with my family daily, gathering around the dinner table each evening.*

- *I cherish my parents and family dearly, showering them with love, trust, and understanding every chance I get.*

- *Surprising my family with little gestures of love brings me immense joy and satisfaction.*

For "completing Amazon Web Services (AWS) certification":

- *Thank you, Universe, for blessing me with a fulfilling software development career where I learn and grow daily!*

- *Diving into the world of technology fills me with excitement and passion.*

- *Today is 18th Sept 2025, and I'm bursting with pride because I achieved my AWS certification a month ago. What an incredible accomplishment!*

- *I thrive on continuous learning and am thrilled to be taking the next step in my professional journey.*

For "having 15 multiple sources of income (MSIs)":

- *Thank you for showering me with abundant financial blessings and opportunities!*

- *My heart is brimming with gratitude for my current wealth and abundance.*

- *Today is 10th Jan 2025, and I am beaming with confidence and security as I celebrate having 15 multiple sources of income. What a remarkable achievement!*

- *Money flows to me effortlessly from every direction, big or small, and I welcome it with open arms.*

- *I am a magnet for wealth, attracting prosperity and abundance into my life with ease and grace.*

For "conducting value-based webinars and workshops":

- *Thank you for igniting my passion and giving me the courage to serve others most effectively!*

- *Hosting webinars and workshops fills me with a sense of purpose and fulfillment.*

- *Thank you for the opportunity to empower and inspire others through my work, delivering ten times the value to every attendee.*

- *I deeply value and appreciate the feedback and concerns of my clients and students, striving to serve them better each day.*

- *I take full ownership of my results and outcomes and am committed to delivering excellence in all I do.*

LET'S DO IT - IT'S YOUR TURN NOW

Now is the time for you to prepare your affirmations.

When you're ready, begin crafting your list of positive statements touching every aspect of your life, as shown below.

If you'd like, feel free to e-mail them to me at morisrhonda@gmail.com. I'd be happy to take a look!

Health affirmations:

1) _____

2) _____

3) _____

4) _____

Relationship affirmations:

1) _____

2) _____

3) _____

4) _____

Career affirmations:

1) _____

2) _____

3) _____

4) _____

Money affirmations:

1) _____

2) _____

3) _____

4) _____

- **Forgiveness is Powerful:** Even when someone hurts you deeply, forgiving them, even just a little, can help you find peace within yourself.

- **Positive Self-Talk Works:** Saying kind and positive things to yourself, even when it's hard, can change how you feel and help you heal from painful experiences.

- **Affirmations are Conversations:** Affirmations are simply like having a conversation with yourself, speaking positively, and empowering yourself.

- **Feel, Think, Believe, Act:** Affirmations align your feelings, thoughts, beliefs, and actions as if you've already achieved your desires.

- **Be Specific with Goals:** When crafting affirmations, be specific about what you want to achieve to give your mind a clear direction to focus on.

- **Speak as if it's Already Happened:** Frame your affirmations as if your goals have already been achieved to trick your brain into believing it's possible.

- **Include Positive Emotions:** Add positive emotional words to your affirmations to enhance their effectiveness and reinforce good feelings.

- **Create the Feeling First:** Get yourself into a positive and energetic state before saying your affirmations to make them more powerful.

- **Three Types of Affirmations:** Thank-you affirmations for gratitude, goal frequency affirmations for achieving goals, and action frequency affirmations for taking necessary actions.

- Crafting affirmations tailored to your specific goals and desires can significantly enhance their effectiveness in manifesting positive outcomes in your life.

THE NEXT IMPORTANT STEPS

"You will be a failure until you impress the subconscious with the conviction you are a success. This is done by making an affirmation which 'clicks.'"

- Florence Scovel Shinn

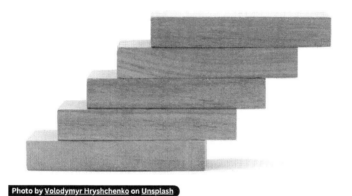

Photo by Volodymyr Hryshchenko on Unsplash

UNDERSTAND THE POTENCY OF YOUR EMOTIONS

I've been immersed in the world of affirmations, manifestation, and the Law of Attraction (LOA) for quite some time now. I've noticed something that's been bothering me through numerous live webinars and training programs. There's a ton of confusion out there, and I believe it's time to clear things up.

Affirmations are all about syncing your vibes with what you want in life and truly feeling as if you already have it. But I've observed that many people are just going through the motions without truly feeling it. It's like they're missing the point entirely.

Take, for example, the desire for a fancy car.

Sure, you can plaster pictures of Ferraris all over your walls and visualize yourself cruising in one, but if you're not feeling that genuine excitement and joy inside, that car isn't going to magically appear in your garage.

Without genuinely feeling the emotions associated with your desires, your affirmations won't have the impact you're hoping for.

As I've emphasized before, the essential elements are **FTBA - feeling, thinking, believing, and acting**. You need to grasp the significance of the emotions tied to your desires. It's about tapping into the emotions you'd experience if you already had what you want. **For instance,** if you're seeking a peaceful home, focus on the feeling of tranquility and serenity rather than just fixating on the physical structure.

Please don't misunderstand me; tools like **gratitude journals** and **vision boards** can be incredibly useful. However, their effectiveness hinges on your ability to genuinely connect with the emotions underlying your desires. It's not merely about going through the motions; it's about feeling it deep in your core.

To really achieve what you affirm in your affirmations, you need to understand the potency of your emotions and use them to align yourself with your desires. **It's not about passively**

wishing for things; it's about immersing yourself in the sensation of already possessing them. That's the real key to making affirmations work for you.

TRUST THE PROCESS & TAKE ACTION

Now that we've covered the affirmation process let's talk about something equally important: **trusting the process.** There are a few things you can do to help your affirmations become a reality. It's essential **not to obsess over the outcome**, but you can certainly set the stage for success.

Imagine planting a seed. You don't need to watch it every second, but you need to plant it in fertile soil to ensure it receives adequate water and sunlight. Similarly, with affirmations, **consider what actionable steps you can take toward achieving your goals**.

For instance, if you're aiming for a career change, start networking and seeking out new job opportunities. If finding love is your goal, be open to meeting new people and saying yes to social events.

Having spent years diving into the world of affirmations, manifestation, and the Law of Attraction (LOA), I've gained invaluable insights from conducting countless webinars and consulting with clients eager to learn the LOA. One theme has remained consistent throughout my journey: **the importance of trusting the process**.

In one memorable consultation session with **Mrs. Simona,** *one of my clients, she expressed frustration with* her affirmations, feeling as though her efforts weren't yielding the desired results.

As our conversation progressed, it became evident that although Mrs. Simona was dedicated to her affirmation practice, she harbored doubts about the effectiveness of the process itself.

Drawing from my own experiences and the principles we've discussed, I shared with Mrs. Simona the analogy of planting a seed.

I emphasized the importance of taking practical steps toward her goals while maintaining a sense of trust and belief in the process. **Just as a seed requires nurturing and time to grow, our affirmations also need space to manifest in our lives**.

I encouraged Mrs. Simona to consider actionable steps she could take toward her desires. In subsequent sessions, she began incorporating gratitude practices into her daily routine, expressing thanks for both current blessings and future manifestations. Over time, she noticed a shift in her mindset and a newfound openness to the opportunities around her.

Through this journey, you can see that I witnessed firsthand **the transformative power of trust in the process!**

HOW SHE CHANGED HER LIFE BY CHANGING HER LIMITING BELIEFS

Once, I had a client from India who was struggling with weight gain and felt deeply disheartened by her increasing weight and lack of control over it. Despite trying various methods like exercise and dieting, nothing seemed to work for her. She expressed her frustration, sharing how her weight gain had impacted her social life, leaving her without marriage proposals and feeling isolated in a dark room, almost like being in a state of depression.

I asked her a simple question during our first conversation: *"What do you think causes your weight gain?"* Her immediate response was alarming—She was suffering from **PCOD** (a hormonal imbalance that affects a woman's ovaries and menstrual health), and she believed that even breathing air caused her to gain weight. This belief came from when she heard from the internet that in PCOD, people gain weight even when they breathe. Despite being untrue, this limiting belief had deeply ingrained itself in her mind, causing her immense frustration and anxiety.

Realizing the power of limiting beliefs, I knew that transforming her mindset and promoting self-love was essential. We began working together twice a week for an hour each session. I introduced her to affirmations to shift her perspective, such as -

"I have already reached my ideal body weight of 155 pounds two months ago. Now I am enjoying my body! I am

eating my favorite food in my favorite restaurant. I love taking care of my health. I love dieting and regular exercise."

Over the next seven months, we witnessed remarkable changes in her mindset and body. By replacing her limiting beliefs with empowering ones, she began to embrace her journey toward health and happiness. Now, she stands at her ideal body weight, savoring life's pleasures, dining at her favorite restaurants, and prioritizing self-love. A simple shift from limiting beliefs to empowering ones has transformed her life, illustrating the profound impact of self-belief and positive affirmation.

ADJUST YOUR BELIEFS

How do you feel when you receive a bill in the mail?

Typically, this isn't something that brings feelings of joy. Instead, it might trigger stress or frustration. But remember, **your thoughts and feelings carry energy**. If you're emitting negative vibes when you see a bill, you're essentially telling the Universe,

"I don't want more money troubles."

So, what can you do differently?

Instead of approaching bills with dread, try shifting your mindset. When you receive a bill, please take a moment to appreciate what it's for. Even if it's for something mundane like electricity or the internet, be grateful for the services it represents. Then, express gratitude to the Universe in advance for providing you with the means to pay for it. This simple change in perspective can transform your relationship with money.

This example shows how tweaking your beliefs can enhance your affirmations. Since your beliefs influence your thoughts and feelings, changing them can shift your entire outlook on money. **And this is not just about money; this holds good for anything you want to improve your relationship with**!

For instance, let's say you're struggling with weight loss. Take some time to reflect on the beliefs you hold about your ability to lose weight. *Are they rooted in reality or based on past experiences or fears?* Challenge these beliefs by separating fact from feeling. Ask yourself if your beliefs are true for everyone or just your perception.

If you think all workplaces are toxic because of your past experiences, **challenge this belief**. Remind yourself that thousands of workplaces are out there, and not all are negative. Reframe your belief to something like,

"There are many great workplaces, and I will find one that suits me."

Let me share **a story from my own life** about how I turned my dream of writing and publishing books into reality.

Back when I started writing, I didn't believe I could make it as an author. I thought success was only for a lucky few, and I was scared of failing. This fear held me back, and I struggled to make progress with my writing.

87

But one day, I decided to change my mindset. I looked at other authors who had faced similar challenges and still succeeded. I started to believe that maybe I could do it, too.

I began practicing affirmations to reinforce this new belief. Every morning, I would repeat affirmations like-

- *I am a brilliant writer overflowing with creativity and inspiration. Every word I write resonates with passion and purpose.*

- *I take consistent action towards my writing goals daily, immersing myself in the joy of the creative process.*

- *I effortlessly achieve my goals with grace and determination. Success is my natural state, and I attract abundance with ease.*

- *Today, on 20th Sept 2026, I am a celebrated author with multiple New York Times best-selling books. My words resonate deeply with readers worldwide, enriching their lives and inspiring positive change. I am grateful for the opportunity to share my wisdom and creativity, bringing immense value to all my dear readers.*

These affirmations helped me to shift my mindset from one of doubt to one of confidence. Instead of letting rejection bring me down, I saw it as a chance to learn and grow. I started to write daily, taking small steps towards finishing my book. I asked for help and feedback from other writers and used their advice to improve my writing.

As I kept working and affirming my belief in myself, things started to change. I finished my first book and found a publisher who liked it. With each book I wrote, I got better and more confident.

Now, I'm proud to say that I've published several books and built a career as an author. It wasn't easy, but **I made my dream come true by changing my beliefs, practicing affirmations, and trusting in myself.**

- **Feel Your Affirmations:** It's not just about saying affirmations; it's about feeling the emotions associated with your desires deeply within yourself. Without genuine emotion, your affirmations may lack potency.

- **Trust the Process:** Trust that your affirmations will manifest, but also take practical steps towards your goals. Like planting a seed, nurturing your affirmations with action helps them grow.

- **Shift Your Beliefs:** Your beliefs shape your reality. If you want to change your life, start by changing your beliefs. Challenge negative beliefs and replace them with positive ones that align with your goals.

- **Gratitude Transforms:** Shift your perspective on things like bills from negative to positive by expressing gratitude for what they represent. This can change your relationship with money and other aspects of life.

- **Separate Fact from Feeling:** Challenge your beliefs by examining whether they're based on reality or past experiences. Reframe them to align with your desires, like changing beliefs about workplaces or weight loss.

- **Consistency is Key:** Consistently practicing affirmations, coupled with action and belief in oneself, can lead to significant personal growth and achievement of goals.

- **Learn and Grow from Challenges:** Instead of letting rejection or challenges bring you down, see them as opportunities to learn and grow. Use feedback to improve and keep moving forward.

- **Success is Possible:** With the right mindset, belief in yourself, and consistent effort, success is achievable.

LET'S IDENTIFY WHY YOUR AFFIRMATIONS ARE STILL NOT WORKING

"My favorite affirmation when I feel stuck or out of sorts is: Whatever I need is already here, and it is all for my highest good. Jot this down and post it conspicuously throughout your home, on your car's dashboard, at your office, on your microwave oven, and even in front of your toilets!"

- Wayne Dyer

Photo by Markus Winkler on Unsplash

In my experience as a mentor and life coach, I've noticed that many people try using affirmations, just like I've explained in earlier chapters. But even though they use the same techniques, they still feel like their affirmations aren't helping them.

Don't worry if you also feel this way; you're not alone.

WHY IT IS NOT WORKING?

In this chapter and the next, I'll explore this topic further and share tips and suggestions about what you can do if nothing works for you. But before we get into that, let's understand why affirmations don't work for some people. Let me explain that first.

- **YOU ARE *'GOING THROUGH THE MOTIONS'* TRAP**

Remember how, back in school, you'd say the Pledge of Allegiance without really thinking about what it meant? It was just something everyone did. Similarly, when you start saying positive affirmations, it might feel like you're making changes at first. But as time passes, they lose their power if you're just repeating them without believing in them.

So, instead of mindlessly repeating affirmations, let's give them some real meaning. Set a reminder to check in on your affirmations regularly, maybe once a month or yearly. Take a moment to ask yourself, *"How has this affirmation actually influenced my actions since the last time I checked?"*

If you can't see any real changes, set a goal related to that affirmation and plan to achieve it. Taking action will give your affirmations more weight and make them feel more meaningful when you say them.

- **YOU *DON'T WANT* YOUR AFFIRMATIONS TO BE TRUE**

Yes, you heard it right! You really don't want your affirmations to be true!

Imagine you've been telling yourself,

"I am healthy and fit, having already shed 44 pounds. "

But when you're faced with the choice of hitting the gym or lounging on the sofa with some pizza, you often choose the pizza. That's because, even though you're saying you want to lose weight, your actions show you might not really want it deep down.

Sometimes, we say positive things about ourselves, but deep down, we might not really want it. Maybe we secretly enjoy eating all the tasty snacks and skipping the gym. It's like saying,

"I want to fit into those skinny jeans, but I also really love pizza nights with friends."

- **YOU ARE *LYING* TO YOURSELF**

Imagine you're trying to convince yourself that you're a great cook. If you burn a batch of cookies and feel terrible because you've let your family down, saying, *"I deeply and completely accept myself as a great cook,"* it might feel genuine. You messed up, but it's okay; you still accept yourself.

Now, picture a different scenario. Let's say you burn those cookies because you were distracted by your phone, and you know you've been neglecting quality time with your loved ones.

In that case, saying the same affirmation might not ring true. You might not accept yourself because you know you've been prioritizing the wrong things.

Similarly, when it comes to affirmations, if you're dealing with regret or shame about something, just saying the words won't cut it. You can't honestly affirm something that clashes with how you truly feel inside. It's like trying to convince yourself you're a great cook when you know you've been slacking. There's resistance because deep down, you know it's not true.

Remember, we humans are good at fooling ourselves. Saying *"Be true to yourself"* sounds simple, but it's tough to do!

- **YOU ARE TRYING TO BE A *PERFECTIONIST***

Once, I was learning to play the piano. I was trying really hard to play each note perfectly, but I forgot to have fun with the music. I kept saying to myself, *"I'm perfect at playing the piano,"* but it only made me feel stressed and worried. The idea of being a perfectionist made it hard for me to believe my affirmations.

Sometimes, when you're always striving for perfection, those positive affirmations you tell yourself don't quite hit the mark. **If you're constantly pushing yourself to be flawless at everything, it's hard to believe those affirmations that say you're doing great**.

It's like trying to grow a flower in tightly packed soil—it just doesn't have room to breathe and grow. So, if you always strive for perfection, maybe it's time to ease up and give yourself some credit. That way, those affirmations can really start to work their magic.

- **YOU ARE NOT GIVING THEM *A FAIR SHOT***

If your day starts with quickly reading through a bunch of positive affirmations. You spend about 5 minutes on this. But then, for the rest of your day—around 16 hours—you keep telling yourself negative stuff like how much of a failure you are or how everything around you is terrible. It's like eating a burnt pizza and pretending it's the best pizza ever.

Don't blame affirmations if they're not working for you if you're not really giving them a fair shot.

So, what does it mean to give affirmations a fair shot?

Well, it's not just about saying them more or trying really hard to believe them. It's about changing your mindset and stopping those negative thoughts in their tracks. If needed, change your actions.

Affirmations aren't magic spells—they're meant to help you change your behaviors from negative to positive. But maybe starting with baby steps is okay. Instead of diving into super positive affirmations, you could start with neutral ones.

For example, instead of saying,

"I'm a fitness fanatic," you could say,

"I'm working on incorporating regular exercise into my routine."

This way, you're not diving headfirst into positive thinking, but you're also not stuck in negative thoughts either. It's like paving a new path in your brain for more positive thinking to follow.

So, if positive affirmations haven't worked for you, why not try **neutral affirmations** when it comes to exercise? Maybe then, sticking to a regular routine will feel much easier.

DO THIS AFFIRMATION EFFECTIVENESS ASSESSMENT

Welcome to the **Affirmations Effectiveness Assessment!** Now is the time to explore your relationship with affirmations to uncover insights into their impact on you through this exercise:

A. Questionnaire:

1. Going Through the Motions:

- *Are you simply going through the motions when saying your affirmations without really believing in them or feeling their meaning?*

  o Yes

  o No

2. Desire for Truth:

- *Do you truly want your affirmations to be true, or are you saying things that don't align with your true desires or beliefs?*

  o Yes, I genuinely want my affirmations to be true.

  o No, my affirmations don't reflect what I truly want.

3. Honesty Check:

- *Are you honest with yourself when saying your affirmations, or are you telling yourself things you don't truly believe?*

  o Yes, I'm being honest with myself.

  o No, I'm lying to myself.

4. Perfectionism Tendency:

- *Are you striving for perfection regarding affirmations setting unrealistic standards for yourself?*

  - Yes, I'm trying to be perfect with my affirmations.

  - No, I understand that perfection isn't necessary.

5. Fair Chance Assessment:

- *Are you giving your affirmations a fair chance to work, or are you dismissing them too quickly?*

  - Yes, I'm giving my affirmations a fair shot.

  - No, I'm not giving my affirmations enough time or effort.

B. Thought-Provoking Questions:

- *What emotions do you experience when saying your affirmations, and do they align with the message you're trying to convey?*

- *Are there any underlying beliefs or fears that might be sabotaging your efforts to embrace positive affirmations?*

- *How do you define success when using affirmations, and are your expectations realistic?*

- *Have you considered how your past experiences and upbringing might influence your receptiveness to affirmations?*

- *Can you identify any patterns or triggers that cause you to doubt or resist affirmations?*

- *Are there alternative approaches or strategies that resonate more with you and might be worth exploring?*

- *How do you talk to yourself when facing challenges or setbacks, and could adjusting your self-talk enhance the effectiveness of your affirmations?*

C. Grading System:

- 5 points for each "Yes" response

- 3 points for each "No" response

D. Grade Interpretation:

- A (20-25 points): You're on the right track with your affirmations! Keep up the positive mindset.

- B (15-19 points): You're making progress, but there's room for improvement. Reflect on your responses and consider adjustments.

- C (10-14 points): There are some barriers hindering the effectiveness of your affirmations. Dive deeper into your mindset and try different approaches. Keep reading the book. You'll find definite solutions.

I hope you answered the questions honestly and discovered where you stand. If you feel like you need to do better, that's okay. You're not alone in this journey. In the upcoming chapters, I'll share tips and tricks to help you improve how you use affirmations. Keep reading, and keep practicing your affirmations!

- **Meaningful Affirmations:** Don't just repeat affirmations mindlessly; check in regularly to see if they're influencing your actions. Set goals related to your affirmations to give them more meaning and weight.

- **Alignment with Desires:** Ensure your affirmations align with your true desires. If your actions don't match your affirmations, it might indicate a deeper conflict between what you say and what you want.

- **Honesty with Yourself:** Be honest when saying affirmations. Affirmations might not feel genuine if you're struggling with regret or shame. Recognize and address these feelings instead of ignoring them.

- **Ease Up on Perfectionism:** Striving for perfection can hinder the effectiveness of affirmations. Give yourself credit for progress and acknowledge that imperfection is part of the journey.

- **Consistency and Balance:** Affirmations require consistent practice and a balanced mindset. Don't dismiss them too quickly or expect instant results. Start with neutral affirmations if positive ones feel overwhelming.

- **Embrace Positive Self-Talk:** Adjust your self-talk when facing challenges or setbacks. Instead of dwelling on negativity, use affirmations to reinforce positive beliefs and behaviors.

- **Continuous Improvement:** Regardless of your assessment score, remember there's always room for improvement. Stay committed to your affirmations journey, and be open to trying new approaches.

- **Community and Support:** You're not alone in this journey. Seek support from mentors, friends, or online communities to share experiences, gain insights, and stay motivated.

- **Persistence and Practice:** Success with affirmations takes time and effort. Keep reading, practicing, and refining your approach.

SO, WHAT TO DO TO MAKE IT WORK?

"By taking massive actions, you breathe life into your affirmations, transforming dreams into tangible achievements."

- Rhonda Morris

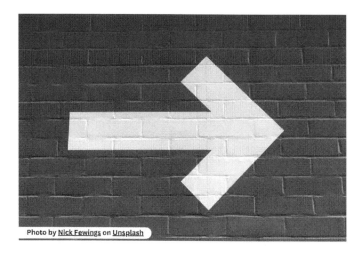

Photo by Nick Fewings on Unsplash

START WITH A CLEAN SLATE

Canadian researcher **Dr. Joanne Wood** and her team at the *University of Waterloo* did a <u>study</u> about saying positive things to yourself. They found something interesting: **when people with low self-esteem were told to repeat a positive affirmation like "I am a lovable person," they actually felt worse afterward. But people with high self-esteem felt better**.

There was something even more interesting:

The researchers asked everyone to think about both good and bad things about themselves. **They found that people with low self-esteem were in a better mood when they were allowed to think negatively about themselves**.

Yeah, you read that right — they felt better when they said bad stuff about themselves.

But why?

The researchers found that it's because - "*Saying positive things didn't match how people with low self-esteem already felt about themselves. It's like trying to fit a square peg into a round hole - it just doesn't work and makes you feel bad. So, instead of feeling good, saying positive things made them feel even worse about themselves.*"

They concluded that ***"repeating positive self-statements may benefit certain people, such as individuals with high self-esteem, but backfire for the very people who need them the most."***

So, if positive affirmations don't work for everyone, what does?

Dr. Joanne suggests that instead of covering up all the negative thoughts with positivity, it might be better to deal with those negative thoughts first, like cleaning out a messy room before trying to decorate it. That way, you start with a clean slate and can build up from there.

Imagine your brain is like a path that your thoughts travel on. Sometimes, these paths can get stuck in negative thinking, like a roadblock that stops you from feeling good about yourself. But, if you introduce some neutral statements—things that are **neither positive nor negative**—and make sure they're **based on reality**, it's like paving a new road in your brain.

Now, here's where my story comes in. Remember when I was writing and publishing my books? At first, maybe I felt like my writing wasn't perfect, or I doubted whether my books would be successful. Those were like the old, negative paths in my brain.

But then, I started to remind myself that it's okay for my writing to be "good enough" for now. I focused on my progress instead of worrying about everything being perfect. That new way of thinking created a stronger foundation for positive thoughts to grow.

So, if you're struggling with negative thoughts that won't go away, try starting with some neutral statements. Give yourself permission to be "good enough" for now, and watch as you slowly but surely start feeling better and better every day.

For example,

1. **Neutral Statements:**

   - Instead of saying, *"I'm the best at everything I do,"* try saying, *"I'm making progress and learning along the way."*

- Instead of saying, *"I'm always happy and confident,"* try saying, *"I have good days and bad days, and that's okay."*

- Instead of saying, *"I never make mistakes,"* try saying, *"I'm capable of learning from my mistakes and growing stronger."*

2. Reality-Based Statements:

- Instead of denying challenges, acknowledge them and then affirm, *"I'm facing challenges, but I'm finding ways to overcome them."*

- Instead of ignoring negative feelings, acknowledge them and then affirm, *"I'm feeling sad right now, but I know this feeling will pass."*

- Instead of pretending everything is perfect, acknowledge imperfections and then affirm, *"I'm a work in progress, and that's perfectly okay."*

3. "Good Enough" Mindset:

Instead of striving for perfection, focus on progress and affirm, *"I'm doing my best, and that's enough for now."*

Instead of expecting immediate results, affirm, *"I'm making small steps forward every day, and that's a success."*

Instead of comparing myself to others, affirm, *"I'm unique and valuable just as I am, and that's enough."*

Once you've cleared your mind, the next big thing to do is **figure out if you have any beliefs holding you back**. Sometimes, without realizing it, you might be stopping yourself from doing things you're capable of, which could make you stronger. These are called **limiting beliefs.**

Let's talk about what they are and how to get past them.

OVERCOME LIMITING BELIEFS

Limiting beliefs are our negative thoughts about ourselves, others, or the world. They're like ideas that hold us back without us even realizing it. They stop us from reaching our goals, chasing our dreams, and being happy. It's really important to notice these beliefs and find ways to get past them to live a better life filled with good things.

Here are a few examples of limiting beliefs:

- *I'm not smart enough to succeed.*

- *I'll never find someone who loves me.*

- *Money is always going to be a struggle for me.*

- *I'm too old to learn something new.*

- *I'll never be as good as [someone else].*

1. Identify your limiting beliefs:

It's like **shining a light on the thoughts that hold you back**. Pay attention to when you feel doubtful or negative about yourself. Write down these thoughts and really look at them.

Are they true, or have you just believed them for a long time?

For example, if you always think, *"I'm not good enough,"* write it down and question if it's really true or just something you've gotten used to thinking.

2. Question Your Limiting Beliefs:

Once you spot those thoughts, it's time to question them.

Ask yourself, *"Is there proof that these thoughts are true?"* Are they based on facts, or are they just guesses?

For instance, if you believe you're too old to learn something new, ask yourself if you've seen others your age do amazing things. Maybe there's proof that age doesn't matter as much as you thought.

3. Flip Your Thoughts with Positive Affirmations:

Now, it's about flipping those negative thoughts on their head. Create positive statements that go against those old beliefs. Repeat these statements every day until they start to feel true.

For example, if you always think,

"I'll never find a job I love," switch it to,

"Thank you, Universe, for blessing me with this wonderful job I landed two months ago. I thoroughly enjoy every

moment and give my best effort. My bosses and colleagues are satisfied with my performance."

Keep saying it until it sinks in.

4. Choose Positive Influences:

It's like choosing the people and things that lift you up instead of bringing you down.

Hang out with friends who encourage you and believe in your dreams. Stay away from folks who make you doubt yourself or agree with your negative thoughts.

Find a mentor or join a group where people support each other and push you to be your best.

Support from my mentor during my tough time:

I remember the time when I first started learning about IoT (Internet of Things); there were times I felt really down and demotivated. I wasn't sure if I could keep going. That's when I turned to my mentor, someone who always boosts my spirits and gives me new energy. He listened to my worries and reminded me of why I started this journey in the first place. His support helped me feel more confident and determined to keep going, even on tough days. Having someone like that by your side can make all the difference.

5. Take Steps Forward

This is where the real magic happens!

Start doing things that challenge your old beliefs. Take small steps toward your goals every day, and don't be afraid to try new things. Whether it's applying for a job you thought was out of reach or signing up for a class you're interested in, taking action helps you prove those old beliefs wrong.

My consistent efforts in writing books:

Take my journey of writing and publishing my book, for example. I had this dream, this idea in my mind, and I believed in it. But it wasn't enough to just believe—I had to take action consistently.

Every day, I dedicated time to write, even when I didn't feel like it. I kept pushing forward, one word at a time, one page at a time. Eventually, all those small steps added up. I finished my book, published it, and achieved my dream. It's proof that consistent action, no matter how small, can lead to big results.

If you take action, you make your affirmations work for you.

1 Identify your limiting beliefs

2 Question Your Limiting Beliefs

3 Flip Your Thoughts with Positive Affirmations

4 Choose Positive Influences

5 Take Steps Forward

You've learned a lot about affirmations - what they are, why they're good for you, and how to make them work. You know about the challenges you might face and how to overcome them, and you understand how limiting beliefs can hold you back.

Now, it's time to put all this knowledge into action. **I recommend practicing self-affirmations every day as part of your routine.** If you're unsure how to create a daily ritual, don't worry! In the next chapter, I'll explain it all. So, stay tuned for more helpful tips!

- **Start with Neutral Statements:** If positive affirmations don't resonate with you, begin with neutral statements that acknowledge reality without judgment. These provide a clean slate for building positive thoughts.

- **Acknowledge Imperfections:** Embrace the concept of being "good enough" and focus on progress rather than perfection. Allow yourself to make mistakes and learn from them.

- **Challenge Limiting Beliefs:** Identify negative thoughts that hinder your progress and question their validity. Replace them with positive affirmations that contradict these limiting beliefs.

- **Take Consistent Action:** Overcome limiting beliefs by taking small steps toward your daily goals. Even in the face of challenges, consistent effort leads to significant progress and success.

LET'S BUILD A DAILY HABIT

"First, forget inspiration. Habit is more dependable. Habit will sustain you whether you're inspired or not."

- Octavia Butler

Photo by Nathan Lemon on Unsplash

As we have seen in the previous chapters, scientists have been studying self-affirmation for many years and found some pretty interesting stuff. It turns out that affirming yourself can really help you deal with stress and challenging times.

But It's not just about saying nice things to yourself. Nope, it's more about digging deep and figuring out what you truly value about yourself.

Effective affirmation **isn't** thinking, *"I want to pump myself up and find ways to say how much I like myself,"* says

David Creswell, a *psychology professor* at *Carnegie Mellon University* who researches self-affirmation. *"It's more about really identifying, in really concrete ways, the kinds of things about you that you really value."*

When you focus on the things you value, it's like putting on a suit of armor. It makes you feel stronger and more confident, so when life throws you a curveball, you're ready to take it on without getting knocked down.

WHY PRACTICE DAILY?

Several researches have shown that telling yourself positive things can really help you deal with challenging situations. Make it a part of your everyday routine. That way, you're building up your resilience and making it easier to handle whatever life throws your way.

1. Staying Resilient

You know how sometimes work can get tough, and you feel like you're under a lot of pressure?

If you make a habit of telling yourself how awesome you are in other parts of your life, like being a great parent or friend, it can actually help you handle those tough situations better.

2. Building a Well-Rounded Life

Ever heard the saying, *"Don't put all your eggs in one basket"?*

Imagine your life is a big basket; each egg represents a different part of who you are - like your family time, hobbies, work, and things you enjoy doing. Now, if you spread your eggs out into different baskets, it's like being involved in lots of different stuff that makes you who you are. Not only does this give you more things to talk about when you're doing your affirmations, but it also helps you feel more balanced and content in your life overall. So, remember to spread those eggs around and enjoy all the different parts of who you are!

3. Valuing What Matters

Ever feel like life is just rushing by, and you're caught up in the chaos of it all?

It happens to the best of us. But when you take a moment to think about the stuff that truly matters to you—like being there for your kids or being a good friend—it's like hitting the pause button. It's a chance to give yourself a high-five for all the awesome things you do. It helps you remember what counts and gives you a sense of direction and meaning amid all the craziness.

So, take a breather and remind yourself of the good stuff— it's like hitting the reset button for your soul.

4. Giving Yourself a Little Boost of Positivity

Ever notice how having a routine can make things feel easier?

When you make affirming yourself a regular part of your day, it builds discipline and makes you feel more in control.

Plus, it takes the guesswork out of what to do first thing in the morning.

5. Feeling in Charge

Life can be full of surprises, right?

But having a morning routine is like creating a little island of predictability in the sea of unpredictability. You can rely on it daily, giving you a sense of control and stability. And let's be honest, who doesn't love feeling like they've got things under control?

6. Getting Stuff Done

You're less likely to waste time dilly-dallying or putting things off when you have a set routine. Instead, you're primed and ready to tackle whatever tasks come your way.

7. Building Healthy Habits

Mornings are a golden opportunity to sneak in some healthy habits. Whether squeezing in a quick workout, whipping up a nutritious breakfast, or spending a few minutes doing affirmations, there's no shortage of ways to kick-start your day positively.

And the best part?

These little habits add up over time, helping you lead a healthier and happier life.

8. Boosting Confidence

Finishing your morning routine isn't just a box to check off—it's **a mini victory**.

And that feeling of accomplishment?

It sticks with you all day long, giving you a little pep in your step and a boost of confidence. So, by starting your day on the right foot, you're not just setting yourself up for success in the morning—you're building a foundation for a life you can be proud of.

EFFECTS OF AFFIRMATIONS ON YOUR MORNING

Think of affirmations like a roadmap for your day—they set the tone and direction. These simple but powerful phrases guide your thoughts and feelings, giving you focus, positivity, and inner strength. It's like having your own personal cheerleader cheering you on each morning.

For instance, saying,

"I am strong and ready for anything" can help you feel empowered and prepared to tackle whatever comes your way.

Or how about

"Today is full of chances, and I am ready for them"?

This affirmation fills you with positivity and openness to new opportunities. And then there's

"I choose happiness, thankfulness, and positivity today," which reminds you that you can choose a positive outlook no matter what.

Starting your day with affirmations can have a significant impact. They shape how you approach your day, interact with others, and feel about yourself. So, incorporating affirmations into your morning routine is a simple yet effective way to set yourself up for a positive and productive day ahead.

7 TIPS TO ADD SELF-AFFIRMATIONS INTO YOUR DAILY ROUTINE

Starting something new can feel pretty scary, right?

But, often, the toughest bit is just taking that first step. Once you do, it gets way easier. You don't need to rearrange your whole day to start giving yourself some positive vibes. Nope!

Self-affirmations are super flexible. You can do them whenever, wherever.

Brushing your teeth? Boom, say an affirmation. Brewing your morning coffee? Yep, say one then, too. Riding the elevator to your desk? Absolutely, affirm away. It's seriously that simple!

Self-affirmation can totally be part of your meditation or mindfulness routine. But remember that - ***"what you do matters too."*** If you want to really believe in those affirmations, try acting in a way that matches them. It's like giving your beliefs a little extra oomph.

Dattilo has rightly said, *"We see ourselves through our behavior better than we see ourselves through our thoughts. When our choices align with our values and the things we want to believe about ourselves, we're moving further along that believability continuum."*

Affirmations are like little daily boosts for your mood and mindset. They work best when you do them every single day. But **don't sweat it!** There are loads of **simple ways to sneak affirmations into your routine** without breaking a sweat. Seriously, it's as easy as pie! Just find what works for you and stick with it. You got this!

I've been sharing **#7 tips** with all my clients to help them add affirmations to their daily routines. Let me explain them here:

Tip #1: Start with Baby Steps

Often, when we want to make a change in our lives, we go all in and set lofty goals. But **starting small and simple can be much more effective**.

Let's say you want to boost your self-esteem with affirmations. Instead of overwhelming yourself with a long list of affirmations to recite daily, incorporate them into your existing routines.

For example, while you're getting ready in the morning, look at yourself in the mirror and say, *"I am confident and capable."* Or, when you're stuck in traffic, remind yourself, *"I am patient and calm."*

By integrating affirmations into your daily activities, you **make them a natural part of your routine,** which increases the likelihood of sticking with them in the long run.

Tip #2: Record and Replay

In today's fast-paced world, finding quiet time for reflection can be challenging. That's where recording your affirmations comes in handy. Imagine you have a hectic schedule and can't find a moment to sit down and practice affirmations. Instead, you can record yourself saying affirmations and listen to them while you're on the go. Whether you're driving, cooking, or exercising, you can easily incorporate affirmations into your day without needing to set aside dedicated time for them.

Tip #3: Boost Your Mood with Music

Music has the power to uplift our spirits and change our moods. Creating a playlist filled with motivational songs can enhance the effects of your affirmations.

Let's say you're feeling a bit down and need a *pick-me-up.* You can listen to your empowering playlist while you're out for a walk or doing chores around the house. Combining uplifting lyrics and positive affirmations can work wonders for your mindset and overall well-being.

Tip #4: Integrate Affirmations into Everyday Habits

We all follow daily routines without even thinking about them, like brushing our teeth or commuting to work. These habits provide the perfect opportunity to incorporate affirmations.

For instance, you can recite affirmations while brushing your teeth or waiting for the bus. By associating affirmations with existing habits, you make them a seamless part of your daily life.

Tip #5: Capture Moments of Inspiration

Inspiration can strike at any moment, whether admiring a beautiful sunset or witnessing a random act of kindness. Whenever you come across something that inspires you or evokes positive emotions, please take a photo of it. These photos serve as visual reminders of the things that bring you joy and remind you of your goals and aspirations.

Tip #6: Regularly Refresh Your Affirmations

As you grow and evolve, your goals and priorities may change. That's why it's important to regularly update your affirmations to reflect your current desires and beliefs.

For example, if you've achieved a goal or overcome a challenge, you may want to replace old affirmations with new ones that align with your current aspirations.

Tip #7: Document Your Journey with Journaling

Journaling is a powerful tool for self-reflection and personal growth. By writing down your affirmations and documenting your thoughts and feelings, you create a record of your journey toward self-improvement.

You can also use journaling to express gratitude, track your progress, and celebrate your successes along the way. Whether you prefer to write in a traditional journal or use a digital app, journaling can help reinforce the positive effects of your affirmations and keep you focused on your goals.

I hope you now understand why practicing affirmations every day is important and how they can positively affect your mornings. I believe that the **seven tips** I shared on adding self-affirmations to your daily routine can help you achieve this.

So, why wait? Let's make a commitment to include affirmations in our daily lives.

Curious about my daily routine?

Stay tuned for the following chapters, where I'll share the routine I've been following for years.

- **Focus on Core Values:** Effective self-affirmation involves identifying and reinforcing the qualities and values you genuinely cherish about yourself. It's about building inner strength and confidence based on what truly matters to you.

- **Balance and Well-Roundedness:** Diversify your affirmations to reflect the various aspects of your life, creating a sense of balance and contentment. Spread your focus across different areas to enjoy a fulfilling and well-rounded existence.

- **Finding Meaning Amid Chaos:** Pause to acknowledge and appreciate the significant aspects of your life amidst the chaos. Reflecting on what truly matters provides direction, purpose, and a sense of fulfillment.

- **Establishing a Morning Routine:** A consistent morning routine, including affirmations, cultivates discipline, control, and stability. It sets a positive tone for the day, fostering confidence and productivity.

- **Cultivating Healthy Habits:** Morning affirmations complement healthy habits, such as exercise and nutritious eating, contributing to overall well-being and happiness.

- **Aligning Behavior with Beliefs:** Act in ways that align with your affirmations to reinforce their credibility and effectiveness. Your actions speak louder than words and strengthen your belief in your affirmations.

- **Flexibility and Consistency:** Incorporate affirmations seamlessly into your daily activities, leveraging various techniques such as recording, music, and habitual integration. Consistency is key to reaping the benefits of affirmations in your life.

25 ESSENTIAL TOOLS FOR YOUR AFFIRMATION JOURNEY

"Your beliefs become your thoughts, Your thoughts become your words, Your words become your actions, Your actions become your habits, Your habits become your values, and Your values become your destiny."

- Mahatma Gandhi

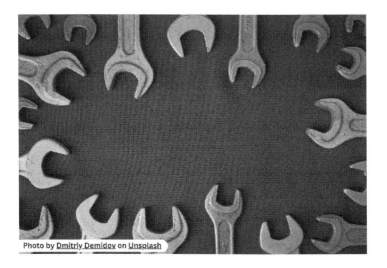

Photo by Dmitriy Demidov on Unsplash

1. Journal or Notebook:

Imagine this as having your own unique book where you can write down everything that's on your mind. You can jot down your feelings and thoughts and even make positive statements or affirmations to boost your mood.

It's kind of like having a personal diary where you can look back on what you've written to see how you've been doing and how far you've come on your journey of self-improvement.

It's a great way to keep track of your progress and reflect on all the steps you've taken towards your goals.

2. Pen or Pencil:

You need something to write with! Whether it's a pen or a pencil, having a writing tool allows you to put your thoughts onto paper in your journal or notebook.

3. Smartphone or Tablet

Think of your smartphone or tablet as a super helpful tool in your affirmation journey. You can use it to access apps that offer affirmations, which are like little pockets of positivity you can carry around with you wherever you go.

Plus, you can record your own voice saying affirmations so you can listen to them whenever you need a boost. And if you want to learn more about staying positive and improving yourself, you can read articles and resources right on your device.

It's like having a whole library of inspiration right at your fingertips!

4. Voice Recording App or Device

Think of a voice recording app or device as your personal cheerleader. Sometimes, hearing positive words spoken aloud can really lift your spirits, right? That's where this tool comes in handy.

You can use it to record yourself saying affirmations in your own voice. Then, whenever you're feeling down or need some encouragement, you can play back those recordings and remind yourself of all the good things you believe about yourself. Plus, you can also find pre-recorded affirmations to listen to whenever you need a quick pick-me-up.

It's like having a supportive friend in your pocket, ready to lift you up whenever you need it.

5. Affirmation Cards or Sticky Notes:

Imagine having little notes scattered around your home or office, each one filled with positivity and encouragement. That's what affirmation cards or sticky notes are all about.

They're like mini reminders to help keep you feeling motivated and upbeat throughout the day. These notes usually have short, positive messages or affirmations written on them, like *"You are capable"* or *"You are enough."*

You can stick them on your mirror, your desk, or anywhere else you'll see them often, so they can give you a little boost whenever you need it.

6. Inspirational Books or Quotes

Surrounding yourself with positive vibes can make a big difference in how you feel.

Picture yourself curled up with a book that's filled with stories of courage, resilience, and hope. Or maybe you have a favorite quote that always makes you feel inspired and motivated.

These books and quotes can be like little bursts of sunshine on a cloudy day, lifting your spirits and reminding you that you can overcome any challenge. They're a great way to keep yourself motivated and focused on your goals.

7. Meditation Cushion or Chair

It's like having a special place just for you to unwind and focus on your affirmations. Whether you prefer sitting on a cushion on the floor or snuggling up in a comfy chair, the important thing is to find a spot where you can feel calm and centered.

This tool helps you create a peaceful environment where you can fully immerse yourself in your affirmations and let go of any distractions.

8. Relaxing Music or Nature Sounds

Sometimes, a little background sound can really set the mood for your affirmation practice.

Imagine listening to soft music playing in the background or hearing the gentle sound of birds chirping outside your window. These sounds help create a soothing atmosphere that makes it easier to relax and focus on your affirmations. It's like setting the stage for a peaceful and rejuvenating experience.

So, find the sounds that resonate with you and let them help you create the perfect ambiance for your affirmation journey.

9. Vision Board or Poster Board

A vision board is a visual representation of your goals and dreams. You can cut out images from magazines, print out quotes that inspire you, and write down affirmations that remind you of what you want to achieve. Then, you put them all together on a board where you can see them every day. It's like having a visual reminder of your dreams and goals right before you.

This tool helps you stay focused and motivated, reminding you of what you're working towards and why it's important to you.

10. Mirror for Self-Reflection

Think about how you feel when you look in the mirror. That reflection staring back at you is a powerful reminder of who you are and your capabilities. That's why using a mirror for self-reflection during your affirmation practice can be so impactful.

It's like having **a one-on-one conversation with yourself,** where you speak words of encouragement and positivity. When you look in the mirror and recite affirmations, you reinforce positive self-talk and boost your self-confidence.

It's a simple but effective way to remind yourself of your worth and potential. So, next time you're feeling down, take a look in the mirror and remind yourself of all the amazing things you have to offer.

11. Timer or Alarm Clock

A timer or alarm clock can help you stay on track and ensure you're giving yourself the time and attention you need.

It's like setting a reminder for yourself to take a moment and focus on your affirmations. By dedicating specific time to your practice, you ensure that you're giving yourself the attention and care you deserve.

Whether it's a few minutes in the morning or before bed, having a timer or alarm helps you stay consistent and committed to your affirmation routine.

12. Affirmation Apps or Websites

Think of affirmation apps or websites as your digital companions on your affirmation journey. You can explore different resources and find ones that resonate with you.

Whether you prefer guided meditations to help you relax or daily affirmations to boost your mood, these apps and websites offer a variety of tools to support you along the way. They're like having a personal coach in your pocket, ready to inspire and motivate you whenever you need it.

13. Gratitude Journal

Practicing gratitude alongside affirmations can help shift your mindset towards a more positive outlook. Each day, you take a moment to write down things you're thankful for, whether it's big or small.

By practicing gratitude alongside affirmations, you shift your mindset towards a more positive outlook. This journal becomes a place to reflect on all the good things in your life and cultivate a sense of abundance and joy.

It's like planting seeds of positivity that grow stronger with each entry.

14. Affirmation Meditation Scripts or Recordings:

Imagine having a gentle voice guiding you through a calming meditation while also reinforcing positive thoughts and beliefs. They're like having a friendly guide walk you through a relaxation session while also reminding you of your inner strength and worth.

These scripts or recordings incorporate affirmations seamlessly into the meditation practice, making it easier for those who prefer a more structured approach to meditation.

Whether you're a beginner or an experienced meditator, these guided sessions can help you cultivate a sense of peace and positivity in your life.

15. Positive Affirmations List or Guide

A list of positive affirmations can be a helpful reference when you're unsure what to say. Think of a positive affirmations list or guide as your go-to source for uplifting and empowering statements.

It's like having a cheat sheet filled with powerful affirmations that you can use whenever you need a boost. You can choose affirmations that resonate with you and align with your goals and values.

Plus, you can use the guide to help you create your own personalized affirmations that reflect your unique journey and aspirations.

16. Affirmation Calendar

A calendar dedicated to affirmations allows you to schedule specific times for your practice and track your consistency over time.

It's like setting appointments with yourself to prioritize your mental and emotional well-being. By scheduling regular affirmation sessions, you ensure that you're giving yourself the time and attention you need to cultivate a positive mindset.

Plus, tracking your consistency over time helps you stay accountable and motivated to stick with your practice. It's like having a visual reminder of your commitment to self-care and personal growth.

17. Affirmation Bracelets or Jewelry

These accessories are like little reminders of your goals and intentions, right there with you throughout the day. They might have engraved affirmations, like *"I am strong"* or *"I am worthy,"* or they might feature symbols representing your aspirations. By wearing them, you're constantly reminded of your inner strength and the path you're on.

It's like having a personal cheerleader with you wherever you go, boosting your confidence and keeping you focused on your journey.

18. Affirmation Posters or Prints

Picture surrounding yourself with positive messages and affirmations right in your own home or office. These are like little bursts of motivation and inspiration that you can hang up in prominent places where you'll see them daily.

They might have affirmations written on them, like *"Believe in yourself"* or *"You are capable,"* or they might feature uplifting images that resonate with you. By surrounding yourself with these positive reminders, you create an environment that supports and encourages you on your journey.

19. Guided Meditation Apps or Recordings

Guided meditation sessions can help you relax and focus while incorporating affirmations into your practice. Look for apps or recordings that align with your goals and preferences.

20. Mindfulness Bell or Chime

Using a mindfulness bell or chime is like having your own personal coach guiding you through your affirmation practice. It's not just a sound—it's a powerful signal that it's time to dive deep into your affirmations and unleash your inner strength.

Hearing that bell or chime is like a call to action, a reminder to bring your full focus and energy to the present moment.

Think about it like this: every time you hear that sound, you create a sacred ritual where you set aside everything else and dedicate yourself fully to your affirmations. It's about more than just saying the words; it's about immersing yourself in them, feeling their power reverberate through your entire being.

21. Affirmation Workshops or Classes

Attending workshops or classes focused on affirmations and positive thinking can provide you with new techniques, insights, and support from others on a similar journey.

22. Nature Walks or Outdoor Spaces

Spending time in nature is like hitting the reset button for your soul. Picture yourself surrounded by the beauty of the natural world—the whisper of the wind, the rustle of leaves, the warmth of the sun on your skin. In these moments, my friend, you can truly connect with yourself and the Universe.

Nature has a way of grounding us, bringing us back to our roots, and reminding us of what truly matters. And in this tranquil setting, practicing affirmations and meditation can take on a whole new level of power and significance.

23. Affirmation Podcasts or Audiobooks

Listening to podcasts or audiobooks that discuss affirmations, personal growth, and mindset can inspire and guide your journey.

24. Affirmation Groups or Communities

Joining a group or community of like-minded individuals who are also on a journey of self-improvement and positivity can provide you with support, encouragement, and accountability.

25. Affirmation Retreats or Retreat Centers

Consider attending a retreat or visiting a retreat center focused on mindfulness, meditation, and affirmations to immerse yourself in a supportive and transformative environment.

My friend, as we draw the curtains on this chapter of your affirmation journey, remember that you hold the power to transform your life within you. Each tool we've explored together is like a key, unlocking the door to your fullest potential.

From affirmation bracelets to guided meditation apps, from gratitude journals to nature walks, each tool serves as a beacon of light, guiding you on your path to greatness.

But it's not just about having these tools—it's about using them with intention, purpose, and a relentless commitment to your growth and happiness.

So, as you move to the next chapter of your journey, I urge you to carry these tools with you, not just in your hands but in your heart. Let them constantly remind you of your strength, courage, and unwavering determination to create the life you deserve.

I hope this list of tools proves helpful, allowing you to have them handy whenever you need them.

As promised, I'm sharing my daily routine with you in the next chapter. Let's proceed...

- Writing down your thoughts and affirmations in a journal helps you reflect on your progress and stay focused on your goals.

- Drawing inspiration from books, quotes, and stories of resilience keeps you motivated and nurtures a positive mindset.

- **Maintaining Consistency with Timers:** Using timers ensures regular affirmation practice, helping you consistently prioritize your mental and emotional well-being.

- Utilizing a mirror for self-reflection reinforces positive self-talk and boosts self-confidence, serving as a potent reminder of your worth and potential.

- Affirmation apps, websites, and guided meditations provide digital support and guidance, offering a variety of tools to inspire and motivate.

- Affirmation meditation scripts or recordings seamlessly integrate affirmations into meditation practice, guiding you toward relaxation and inner strength.

MY DAILY ROUTINE

"Not only is procrastination bad because it makes us less efficient, but it can also ruin the entire notion of building a habit in the first place."

- J. J. Thomas

Photo by Tim Foster on Unsplash

*I*n the gentle embrace of the early morning, I welcome the **Divine Time,** a sacred moment to connect with the sweetness of the Universe. As the dawn breaks, I awaken between 4-5, feeling the **energy of the Universe** flowing through me. **Gratitude** fills my heart, and I offer thanks for **ten blessings**, feeling the love and abundance that surrounds me.

I perform the **Mai Yur Ma** ritual with love and intention, **symbolizing unconditional love and goodwill** and *invoking positivity for the day ahead. In the quiet of* **meditation,** *I find peace for twenty minutes, allowing my mind to settle and my spirit to soar. As the morning light bathes me in warmth, I* **chant affirmations 108 times,** *affirming* **health, love, abundance, and success** *in all aspects of my life.*

Stepping outside into **nature's embrace,** *I take a leisurely walk, soaking in the beauty of the early morning sun and the refreshing breeze. In harmony with the rhythm of nature, I prepare breakfast and nourishing meals for the day ahead, infusing each dish with love and gratitude.*

Throughout my day's journey, I remain **mindful** *of the blessings bestowed upon me. With my* **magical water bottle** *by my side, I stay hydrated, grateful for the gift of life and vitality. I deposit* **a gratitude note in my jar,** *capturing the small miracles that unfold each day. In my* **magical diary,** *I record the wonders of the Universe, celebrating the magic that surrounds me.*

In moments of challenge, I turn to **EFT, self-affirmations,** *and* **"cancel-cancel" techniques,** *releasing negativity and embracing positivity. With a heart open to giving, I aspire to be a channel of blessings for others, spreading love and kindness wherever I go.*

My aim remains: **"MAY I BE THE CHANNEL OF BLESSINGS FOR SOMEONE TODAY!"**

As the evening descends, I cherish **precious moments with my family,** *sharing laughter, dreams, and quiet* moments of togetherness. With each **evening walk,** I reflect on the day's blessings, grateful for the gift of health and vitality.

Entering the realm of nighttime, I immerse myself in **value-based webinars** and **workshops,** feeding my mind and soul with **wisdom** and **inspiration.** Together with my coach and fellow seekers, we practice the **Daily Magic Practice, affirming health, love, abundance, and success as one.**

In the quiet hours before sleep, I nurture my passion for writing, pouring my heart onto the page as I embark on the journey of **author-preneurship.** With gratitude in my heart, I release all that no longer serves me, surrendering to the loving embrace of the Universe as I drift into peaceful slumber.

BONUS CHAPTER - 100 READY-MADE AFFIRMATIONS TO PRACTICE

"Today, many will choose to free themselves from the personal imprisonment of their bad habits. Why not you?"

- Steve Maraboli

Photo by Jess Bailey on Unsplash

25 HEALTH AFFIRMATIONS

1. Thank you for the vibrant health and boundless energy I experience every day.

2. Every action I take aligns with my commitment to nurturing my body and mind.

3. I prioritize self-care daily, knowing it is the key to my long-term health and happiness.

4. I am continuously attracting opportunities to enhance my health and vitality.

5. Thank you for the joy and fulfillment that comes from living a healthy lifestyle.

6. I am attuned to my body's needs, providing it with nourishment and care, and I am grateful to the Universe for this connection.

7. I am surrounded by love and support that nourishes my mind, body, and soul.

8. I am becoming stronger, healthier, and more vibrant each day, increasing my stamina and endurance by [specific measure] percent.

9. I celebrate my body's ability to heal and rejuvenate itself, maintaining an ideal weight of <<write_your_number>> pounds.

10. With heartfelt thanks to the Universe, my immune system is powerful and resilient, protecting me from illness and disease effortlessly.

11. I am worthy of investing time and effort into my health and well-being, achieving <<write_your_number>> hours of quality sleep every night.

12. I choose thoughts and actions that promote my physical and mental health, engaging in <<write_your_number>> minutes of exercise daily.

13. Each organ and internal system in my body functions harmoniously, supporting my overall well-being; I am grateful to the Universe for this balance.

14. My body is a temple, and I treat it with the utmost care and respect, consuming a balanced diet daily.

15. I am filled with gratitude for the gift of life and the opportunity to experience good health, maintaining my blood pressure at <<write_your_number>> over <<write_your_number>>.

16. I am grateful for the opportunity to care for my body and nurture my soul, practicing self-care rituals every day.

17. I trust in my body's ability to heal itself and maintain perfect health, keeping my cholesterol levels balanced.

18. With gratitude to the Universe, my knees are strong and flexible, allowing me to move gracefully and effortlessly.

19. I express gratitude to the Universe for my thick, lustrous hair, a reflection of my vibrant health.

20. I breathe easily with clear and strong lungs. Thank you, Universe, for sustaining my breath effortlessly.

21. My bones and joints allow me to move freely and without pain. Thank you, Universe, for their strength and flexibility.

22. My mind is sharp and focused, capable of clear thinking and creative expression; thank you, Universe, for this clarity.

23. My body heals itself with love and care every day. Thank you, Universe, for this innate ability.

24. My skin is radiant and clear, reflecting the vibrant health of my entire being, and I am grateful to the Universe for this glow.

25. My eyesight is clear and sharp, enabling me to see the beauty in the world around me; I am grateful to the Universe for this clarity of vision.

25 RELATIONSHIP AFFIRMATIONS

1. I am worthy of love and respect, and I treat myself with kindness and compassion daily.

2. Thank you for the deep love and understanding I have for myself, nurturing a strong foundation for all my relationships.

3. I attract and maintain healthy and fulfilling relationships in all areas of my life.

4. I communicate openly and authentically, deepening my connections with others.

5. I set clear boundaries that honor my needs and values, fostering respect and mutual understanding in my relationships.

6. I am committed to resolving conflicts peacefully and constructively, fostering harmony and unity in my relationships.

7. I am worthy of love and respect, attracting supportive and nurturing relationships into my life.

8. I invest time and effort in building and maintaining meaningful connections, creating a network of love and support around me.

9. I engage in self-care practices that nurture my well-being and strengthen my relationships.

10. I seek opportunities to show kindness and generosity to others, enriching their lives and mine.

11. I prioritize spending quality time with my family creating cherished memories and experiences together.

12. I continuously invest in personal growth and self-awareness, enriching my relationships with authenticity and depth.

13. I actively listen and empathize with others, cultivating deeper connections and understanding.

14. I communicate my needs and desires openly and assertively, fostering healthy and balanced relationships.

15. I prioritize quality time with my loved ones, strengthening our bonds of love and friendship.

16. I embrace my uniqueness and celebrate all that makes me who I am, appreciating myself fully.

17. I am grateful for the joy and companionship my spouse brings into my life, cherishing each moment we share together.

18. Our communication is open and honest, allowing us to resolve conflicts peacefully and further strengthen our connection.

19. I prioritize spending quality time with my parents daily, cherishing each moment we share and nurturing our bond.

20. My heart is filled with love and appreciation for my parents, and I actively seek ways to show them how much they mean to me through gestures of kindness and affection.

21. I recognize the importance of family dinners in fostering a sense of unity and connection, and I prioritize gathering with my parents each week to share a meal and meaningful conversation.

22. I delight in giving thoughtful gifts to my parents, expressing my love and gratitude for their presence in my life, and receiving their blessings in return.

23. I consistently strive to give my best effort in all tasks and projects, contributing positively to my team's success and earning my boss's trust and respect.

24. I cultivate a positive and healthy relationship with my boss, fostering open communication and mutual respect.

25. I actively contribute to a supportive and collaborative environment with my colleagues, fostering positivity and productivity in our workplace.

25 CAREER AFFIRMATIONS

1. I excel in my role, consistently exceeding expectations and delivering exceptional results.

2. I am respected and valued in my workplace for my expertise, dedication, and contributions.

3. I am on the path to achieving my career goals, with each day bringing me closer to success.

4. I am confident in my abilities and skills, knowing that I have what it takes to reach the pinnacle of my career.

5. I am a dynamic and innovative professional, continuously seeking opportunities for growth and advancement.

6. I prioritize self-care and well-being, maintaining a healthy balance between work and personal life.

7. I set boundaries that honor my time and energy, ensuring that I have the space to recharge and rejuvenate.

8. I am efficient and productive in my work, allowing me to accomplish tasks effectively and enjoy quality time with loved ones.

9. I embrace flexibility and adaptability, finding creative ways to manage my workload while nurturing relationships and pursuing hobbies.

10. I build strong and authentic connections with my clients, earning their trust and loyalty through integrity and reliability.

11. I listen attentively to my clients' needs and concerns, offering solutions and support that exceed their expectations.

12. I communicate with clarity and professionalism, ensuring that my clients feel valued and understood at every interaction.

13. I anticipate and address challenges proactively, demonstrating my commitment to delivering exceptional service and results.

14. I am grateful for the opportunity to work with my clients, and I approach each interaction with gratitude and positivity.

15. I am a magnet for exciting career opportunities, effortlessly attracting positions that align with my skills, values, and aspirations.

16. I showcase my unique talents and experiences with confidence, positioning myself as a top candidate for desirable job openings.

17. I network strategically and authentically, building relationships that open doors to new opportunities and connections.

18. I am open to change and growth, embracing new challenges and experiences that propel my career forward.

19. I prepare thoroughly and thoughtfully for interviews, showcasing my qualifications and achievements with confidence and clarity.

20. I articulate my strengths and experiences effectively, leaving a lasting impression on interviewers and demonstrating my value as a candidate.

21. I approach interviews as opportunities to connect and learn, engaging authentically with interviewers and expressing genuine interest in the role and company.

22. I answer questions with poise and professionalism, demonstrating my expertise and suitability for the position.

23. I am a high-performing and valuable member of my team, deserving of recognition and advancement.

24. Thank you, Universe, for aligning my career path with prosperity and abundance. With my salary now at

$20K, I embrace the joy and fulfillment that comes with financial stability and success.

25. Thank you, Universe, for aligning my career path with growth and opportunity. As Head Area Manager, I embrace the challenges and responsibilities that come with leading and managing a team.

25 MONEY AFFIRMATIONS

1. My <<write_your_number>> money target is already achieved, and I celebrate the abundance that flows into my life.

2. I am on track to reaching my financial goals effortlessly and with ease.

3. I am worthy of wealth and abundance and embrace my inherent power to manifest financial success.

4. Thank you, Universe, for guiding me towards financial success and achieving my money target.

5. I deserve financial abundance and attract wealth into my life with every thought and action.

6. I release all limiting beliefs and fears surrounding money, allowing abundance to flow freely into my life.

7. I am worthy of financial security and prosperity, and I release any past struggles with money with gratitude and forgiveness.

8. I trust that abundance is my birthright, and I let go of any scarcity mindset that may have held me back in the past.

9. I am grateful for the lessons learned from past financial challenges and embrace them as opportunities for growth and transformation.

10. I am a magnet for money and wealth, attracting abundance into my life effortlessly and consistently.

11. Money flows to me easily and abundantly, allowing me to live a life of abundance and fulfillment.

12. I am open and receptive to all forms of abundance and welcome wealth into my life with open arms.

13. I am financially secure and stable, with my needs and desires abundantly met.

14. I trust in the Universe to provide for me and support me in all financial matters, ensuring my continued prosperity.

15. I am grateful for the abundance that flows into my life, providing me with everything I need and more.

16. I am a conscious creator of my financial reality and committed to manifesting wealth and abundance in every aspect of my life.

17. I am financially free and independent, with the ability to live life on my own terms.

18. I release any attachments to financial limitations and embrace the limitless abundance of the Universe.

19. I embody a wealth mindset, attracting prosperity and abundance into every area of my life.

20. Thank you, Universe, for blessing me with a wealth mindset that attracts limitless abundance into my life.

21. I radiate confidence and positivity, knowing that I am a magnet for wealth and abundance in all its forms.

22. I am grateful for the abundance of opportunities that have allowed me to establish 15 multiple sources of income effortlessly.

23. I celebrate the 35% increase in my net worth from the previous month, grateful for the abundance that flows into my life.

24. I effortlessly manifest four international trips in business class every year, indulging in luxury and comfort as I explore the world.

25. My shares and investments are increasing exponentially, providing me with a sense of financial stability and security.

CONCLUSION

Photo by Saffu on Unsplash

*C*ongratulations on reaching the end of this *transformative journey!*

I extend my warmest embrace and deepest admiration for your commitment to self-discovery and growth. By persevering through each chapter, you have demonstrated an unwavering dedication to unlocking your infinite potential.

Throughout this book, we have delved into the profound essence of affirmations, unraveling their intricate tapestry and revealing their profound impact on our lives. From understanding their origins and rise to exploring the profound connection between affirmations and success, health, and overall well-being, we have embarked on a journey of self-awareness and empowerment.

You have embraced the wisdom of the ages and the cutting-edge insights of modern science, recognizing the undeniable truth that **affirmations are not merely words but powerful tools for transformation.** Armed with this knowledge, you have learned to harness the full potential of affirmations to **manifest your deepest desires and aspirations.**

Knowing + Not Doing = Not Knowing.

As we conclude this enlightening odyssey, now is the time to **implement.** If you know something but don't implement it, it's like not knowing. Knowing + Not Doing = Not Knowing. Embrace the **golden rules of crafting powerful affirmations** and let them serve as guiding beacons on your continued journey of self-discovery.

Remember, dear reader, that the magic of affirmations lies in their words and the unwavering belief and intention behind them. **With every** *"thank you," "I am,"* **and** *"I can,"* **you are affirming your innate power to shape your reality and create the life of your dreams.**

So, as you bid farewell to these pages and embark on the next chapter of your journey, do so with confidence, courage, and unwavering faith in your ability to manifest miracles. **You are** the architect of your destiny, the master of your fate, and the creator of your reality.

May your affirmations continue to illuminate your path, inspire your soul, and lead you closer to fulfilling your deepest desires. I bid you farewell with boundless gratitude and infinite blessings, knowing that the journey ahead is filled with limitless possibilities.

See you in my other book - **Rhonda.**

REFERENCES

Photo by Tom Hermans on Unsplash

I've gained my insights and comprehension of the subject through personal encounters, extensive reading, and exploring numerous websites.

While it's impractical to enumerate them all, I want to extend my gratitude to the following books/websites, which have significantly enriched my understanding:

- blog.innertune.com
- ca.indeed.com
- en.wikipedia.org
- fastercapital.com
- health.clevelandclinic.org
- joshsteimle.com

- journals.sagepub.com
- moraleapp.co
- positivepsychology.com
- psycnet.apa.org
- www.2minuteaffirmations.com
- www.blinkist.com
- www.briantracy.com
- www.everydayhealth.com
- www.healthline.com
- www.huffpost.com
- www.mentalhelp.net
- www.noomii.com
- www.quora.com
- www.sciencedirect.com
- www.washingtonpost.com
- www.youtube.com

DISCLAIMER

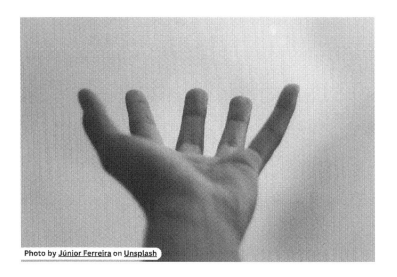

This book, *"Let's Master Affirmations,"* is intended to provide insights and guidance on the practice of affirmations. While affirmations can be a valuable tool for personal growth and self-improvement, it's important to note that the effectiveness of affirmations may vary from person to person.

The information provided in this book is based on personal experiences, research, and observations, and it is not intended to serve as a substitute for professional advice or therapy. It's crucial to consult with qualified professionals, such as therapists or medical professionals, if you have any concerns about your mental or physical health.

Additionally, the success of affirmations depends on various factors, including individual beliefs, consistency in practice, and external circumstances. Therefore, we cannot guarantee specific outcomes or results from using affirmations outlined in this book.

Ultimately, the practice of affirmations should be approached with an open mind and a willingness to explore what works best for you. It's essential to listen to your intuition, take responsibility for your well-being, and make informed decisions aligning with your needs and values.

ABOUT THE AUTHOR

Rhonda Morris is a **bestselling author** and expert in the field of personal development and the Law of Attraction. With a passion for understanding human behavior and empowering others, she has dedicated her career to **helping individuals unlock their full potential** and live their best lives.

Rhonda holds a **Bachelor's degree in Psychology**, a **Master's degree in Counseling, and Computer Science.** Her diverse educational background enriches her approach to personal growth, blending insights from psychology with innovative technological solutions.

As the **founder of the IOT Meeting Hub,** Rhonda is at the forefront of leveraging technology to connect and empower communities. Through this platform, she facilitates collaboration and knowledge sharing among industry professionals, driving innovation and progress in the field of the **Internet of Things.**

With years of experience as **a certified Law of Attraction coach,** she has guided countless individuals on their journey to success and fulfillment. When she's not writing or coaching, Rhonda enjoys spending time outdoors with her family, exploring nature trails, and indulging in her love for gourmet cooking. **Based in sunny California,** she finds inspiration in the beauty of her surroundings and is grateful for the opportunity to make a positive impact on the lives of others.

Connect with Rhonda at morisrhonda@gmail.com

or visit: https://rhondamoris.com

MAY I ASK YOU FOR A SMALL FAVOR?

Photo by Towfiqu barbhuiya on Unsplash

First, I want to say a big thanks for reading this book. You could have chosen any other book, but you took mine, and I appreciate this.

I hope you have at least a few actionable insights that will positively impact your daily life.

Can I ask for 30 seconds more of your time?

I'd love it if you could leave a review of the book. That will help me grow my readership by encouraging folks to take a chance on my books.

It will take less than a minute of your time but will tremendously help me reach out to more people.

If you liked this book, **please consider posting an honest review on your preferred retailer.** And I'd love to see your review. Thanks for your support.

MAY I BE THE CHANNEL OF BLESSINGS FOR SOMEONE TODAY!

Your FREE GIFT

As an expression of gratitude for investing your time in reading my book, I'd like to extend **a complimentary gift** to you. Get this **eBook** to transform your mindset and attract abundance.

Click here or **scan the below QR code** to receive *"1000 Affirmations - The Only Book On Affirmations You Need!"*

Made in United States
Troutdale, OR
08/18/2024